Lecture Notes in Computer Science 11809

More information about this series at http://www.springer.com/series/7409

Jingkuan Song · Xiaofeng Zhu (Eds.)

Web and Big Data

APWeb-WAIM 2019 International Workshops
KGMA and DSEA
Chengdu, China, August 1–3, 2019
Revised Selected Papers

 Springer

Editors
Jingkuan Song
University of Electronic Science
and Technology of China
Chengdu, China

Xiaofeng Zhu
Massey University
Auckland, New Zealand

ISSN 0302-9743   ISSN 1611-3349   (electronic)
Lecture Notes in Computer Science
ISBN 978-3-030-33981-4   ISBN 978-3-030-33982-1   (eBook)
https://doi.org/10.1007/978-3-030-33982-1

LNCS Sublibrary: SL3 – Information Systems and Applications, incl. Internet/Web, and HCI

This Springer imprint is published by the registered company Springer Nature Switzerland AG
The registered company address is: Gewerbestrasse 11, 6330 Cham, Switzerland

Preface

The Asia Pacific Web (APWeb) and Web-Age Information Management (WAIM) Joint Conference on Web and Big Data is a leading international conference for researchers, practitioners, developers, and users to share and exchange their cutting-edge ideas, results, experiences, techniques, and tools in connection with all aspects of Web data management. This third joint event of APWeb and WAIM (APWeb-WAIM 2019) was held in Chengdu, China, during August 1–3, 2019, and it attracted participants from all over the world.

Along with the main conference, APWeb-WAIM 2019 workshops provided an international forum for researchers to discuss and share research results. After reviewing the workshop proposals, we were able to accept two workshops, which focused on topics in knowledge graph and data science. The covered topics in these workshops contributed to the main themes of the APWeb-WAIM conference. For these workshops, we accepted 8 full papers that were carefully reviewed from 18 submissions. The two workshops were as follows:

- The Second International Workshop on Knowledge Graph Management and Analysis (KGMA 2019)
- The First International Workshop on Data Science for Emerging Applications (DSEA 2019)

The workshop program would not have been possible without the authors who chose APWeb-WAIM for disseminating their findings. We would like to thank our authors who improved and extended their papers based on the reviewers' feedback and the discussions held during APWeb-WAIM 2019. We would also like express our thanks to all the workshop organizers for their great effort in making the APWeb-WAIM 2019 workshops a success, and the conference general co-chairs Heng Tao Shen, Kotagiri Ramamohanarao, and Jiliu Zhou, and Program Committee co-chairs Jie Shao, Man Lung Yiu, and Masashi Toyoda for their great support. Volunteers helped with local arrangements and on-site setups, and many other important tasks. While it is difficult to list all their names here, we would like to take this opportunity to sincerely thank them all.

September 2019

Jingkuan Song
Xiaofeng Zhu

Organization

APWeb-WAIM 2019 Workshop Co-chairs

Jingkuan Song	University of Electronic Science and Technology of China, China
Xiaofeng Zhu	Massey University, New Zealand

KGMA 2019

Workshop Co-chairs

Xin Wang	Tianjin University, China
Yuan-Fang Li	Monash University, Australia

Program Committee Members

Gao Cong	Nanyang Technological University, Singapore
Huajun Chen	Zhejiang University, China
Jun Gao	Peking University, China
Armin Haller	Australian National University, Australia
Martin Kollingbaum	University of Aberdeen, UK
Jiaheng Lu	University of Helsinki, Finland
Jianxin Li	Deakin University, Australia
Ronghua Li	Beijing Institute of Technology, China
Jeff Z. Pan	University of Aberdeen, UK
Jijun Tang	University of South Carolina, USA
Haofen Wang	Shanghai Leyan Technologies Co. Ltd, China
Hongzhi Wang	Harbin University of Industry, China
Junhu Wang	Griffith University, Australia
Guohui Xiao	Free University of Bozen-Bolzano, Italy
Zhuoming Xu	Hohai University, China
Qingpeng Zhang	City University of Hong Kong, Hong Kong, China
Xiaowang Zhang	Tianjin University, China
Wei Zhang	Alibaba, China
W. Jim Zheng	The University of Texas Health Science Center at Houston, USA

DSEA 2019

Program Co-chairs

Lianli Gao	University of Electronic Science and Technology of China, China
Han Su	University of Electronic Science and Technology of China, China

| Jiajie Xu | Soochow University, China |
| Zhixu Li | Soochow University, China |

Program Committee Members

Kai Zheng	University of Electronic Science and Technology of China, China
Wen Hua	The University of Queensland, Australia
Bolong Zheng	Huazhong University of Science and Technology, China
Shuo Shang	Inception Institute of Artificial Intelligence, UAE
Guanfeng Liu	Macquarie University, Australia
Yaguang Li	Google, USA
Qing Xie	Wuhan University of Technology, China
Jia Zhu	South China Normal University, China
Lei Li	The University of Queensland, Australia
Jiajun Liu	Renmin University of China, China
Yang Yang	University of Electronic Science and Technology of China, China

Contents

KGMA

Distributed Query Evaluation over Large RDF Graphs

Peng Peng[✉]

Hunan University, Changsha, China
hnu16pp@hnu.edu.cn

Abstract. RDF is increasingly being used to encode data for the semantic web and data exchange. There have been a large number of studies that address RDF data management over different distributed platforms. In this paper we provide an overview of these studies. This paper divide the studies of existing distributed RDF systems into two categories: partitioning-based approaches and cloud-based approaches. We also introduce a partition-tolerant distributed RDF system, gStore^D.

Keywords: Distributed RDF systems · SPARQL query evaluation · Partial evaluation

1 Background

Since Google launched the knowledge graph project at 2012, there are an increasing number of institutes and companies following the project to propose their own knowledge graphs. Essentially, knowledge graph is a semantic network, which models the entities (including properties) and the relation between each other.

Right now, Resource Description Framework (RDF) is the de facto standard of the knowledge graph. RDF is a family of specifications originally designed as a metadata data model. It has also been used in knowledge management applications. Based on the model of RDF, machine in the web can understand the information on it and the interrelationships among them.

In general, RDF represents data as a collection of triples of the form <subject, property, object>. A triple can be naturally seen as a pair of entities connected by a named relationship or an entity associated with a named attribute value. Thus, an RDF dataset can be represented as a graph where subjects and objects are vertices, and triples are edges with property names as edge labels. On the other hand, to retrieve the RDF dataset, a query language SPARQL is designed. A SPARQL query is a set of triple patterns with variables and can be also seen as a query graph with variables. Essentially, answering a SPARQL query requires finding subgraph matches of the query graph over an RDF graph.

Figure 1(a) shows an example RDF graph, which describe some facts about the philosopher Boethius and is a part of a well-known RDF graph, DBpedia [7].

© Springer Nature Switzerland AG 2019
J. Song and X. Zhu (Eds.): APWeb-WAIM 2019 Workshops, LNCS 11809, pp. 3–7, 2019.
https://doi.org/10.1007/978-3-030-33982-1_1

An example query of four edges to retrieve all people influencing people born in Rome is given in Fig. 1(b). After evaluating the query over the RDF graph, we can find out that Cicero and Proclus influence Boethius who is born in Rome.

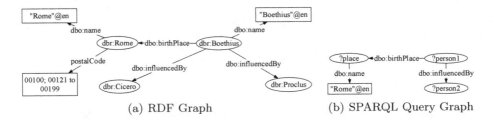

(a) RDF Graph   (b) SPARQL Query Graph

Fig. 1. Example RDF graph and SPARQL query graph

As more and more people publish their datasets in the model of RDF, the sizes of RDF graphs are beyond the capacity of a single machine. For example, YAGO [9] extracted from Wikipedia by Max Planck Institute contains about 284 million triples; Freebase [2], a collaboratively created knowledge graph for structuring human knowledge, contains more than 2 billion triples; DBpedia [7] extracted from Wikipedia by multiple institute contains more than 9 billion triples. Thus, designing a distributed RDF database system is essential.

In this paper, we provide an overview of some distributed distributed RDF systems. We first present a brief survey of distributed RDF systems and categorize them into two categories in Sect. 2. We further discuss a partition-tolerant distributed RDF system implemented by our labs, named gStore^D, in Sect. 3. Finally, Sect. 4 concludes our findings.

2   Distributed RDF Systems

There have been many distributed RDF systems for distributed SPARQL query evaluation, and two very good surveys are [1,5]. In general, these distributed RDF systems can be divided into two categories: partitioning-based approaches and cloud-based approaches.

2.1   Partitioning-Based Approaches

First, some approaches [4,10,11,16,17] are partitioning-based. They divide an RDF graph into several partitions. Each partition is placed at a site that installs a centralized RDF system to manage it. At run time, a SPARQL query is decomposed into several subqueries that can be answered locally at a site. The results of the subqueries are finally merged.

Specifically, H-RDF-3X [4] uses METIS [6], an well-known balanced vertex partitioning method, to partition the RDF graph and each partition is stored and managed by a centralized RDF system. DiploCloud [17] asks the administrator to define some templates as the partition unit. DiploCloud stores the instantiations of the templates in compact lists as in a column-oriented database system; PathBMC [16] adopts the end-to-end path as the partition unit to partition the data and query graph; and Peng et al. [10,11] mine some frequent patterns in the log as the partitioning units.

2.2   Cloud-Based Approaches

Second, some recent works (e.g., [3,8,14]) focus on evaluating SPARQL queries using cloud platforms.

Stylus [3] uses Trinity [15], a distributed in-memory key-value store, to maintain the adjacent list of the RDF graph while considering the types of vertices. In the online phase, Stylus decomposes the query into multiple star subqueries and evaluates the subqueries by using the interfaces of Trinity. S2RDF [14] and WORQ [8] are two distributed RDF systems built on top of Spark. S2RDF [14] uses Spark SQL to store the RDF data in a vertical partitioning schema and materializes some extra join relations. In the online phase, S2RDF transforms the query into SQL queries. WORQ [8] further proposes two optimizations to optimize the SPARQL query evaluation over the vertical partitioning schema. The first one is to use Bloom filters for optimizing joins, and the second one is to cache some intermediate results based on the quer workload.

3 $gStore^D$: A Partial Evaluation-Based Distributed RDF System

In many applications, the RDF repository partitioning strategy is not controlled by the distributed RDF system itself. There may be some administrative requirements that influence the data partitioning. Therefore, partition-tolerant SPARQL processing may be desirable.

For partitioning-tolerant SPARQL processing on distributed RDF graphs, we propose a distributed RDF system, named gStore^D, to evaluate SPARQL queries in a "partial evaluation and assembly" framework, [12,13]. In gStore^D, an RDF graph is partitioned using some graph partitioning algorithm such as METIS [6] into vertex-disjoint fragments (edges that cross fragments are replicated in source and target fragments). Each site receives the full SPARQL query and executes it on the local RDF graph fragment providing data parallel computation.

The framework of gStore^D is as shown in Fig. 2. There are three steps in gStore^D as follows.

- **Step 1 (Initialization):** A SPARQL query Q is input and sent to each site.
- **Step 2 (Partial Evaluation):** Each site finds local partial matches of Q over its fragment. This step is executed in parallel at each site.
- **Step 3 (Assembly):** Finally, we assemble all local partial matches to compute complete crossing matches.

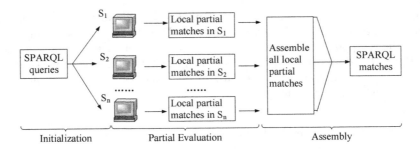

Fig. 2. Framework of gStore^D

4   Conclusions

In this paper, we classify and present a brief overview of systems in each category. There are many additional works on distributed RDF management that are omitted in this paper. Most notably, works on federated RDF systems are topics that are not covered.

Acknowledgment. This work was supported by NSFC under grant 61702171, Hunan Provincial Natural Science Foundation of China under grant 2018JJ3065, and the Fundamental Research Funds for the Central Universities.

References

1. Abdelaziz, I., Harbi, R., Khayyat, Z., Kalnis, P.: A survey and experimental comparison of distributed SPARQL engines for very large RDF data. PVLDB **10**(13), 2049–2060 (2017)
2. Google: Freebase data dumps (2017)
3. He, L., et al.: Stylus: a strongly-typed store for serving massive RDF data. PVLDB **11**(2), 203–216 (2017)
4. Huang, J., Abadi, D.J., Ren, K.: Scalable SPARQL querying of large RDF graphs. PVLDB **4**(11), 1123–1134 (2011)
5. Kaoudi, Z., Manolescu, I.: RDF in the clouds: a survey. VLDB J. **24**(1), 67–91 (2015)
6. Karypis, G., Kumar, V.: Multilevel graph partitioning schemes. In: ICPP, pp. 113–122 (1995)
7. Lehmann, J., et al.: DBpedia - a large-scale, multilingual knowledge base extracted from Wikipedia. Semant. Web **6**(2), 167–195 (2015)
8. Madkour, A., Aly, A.M., Aref, W.G.: WORQ: workload-driven RDF query processing. In: Vrandečić, D., et al. (eds.) ISWC 2018. LNCS, vol. 11136, pp. 583–599. Springer, Cham (2018). https://doi.org/10.1007/978-3-030-00671-6_34
9. Mahdisoltani, F., Biega, J., Suchanek, F.M.: YAGO3: a knowledge base from multilingual Wikipedias (2015)
10. Peng, P., Zou, L., Chen, L., Zhao, D.: Query workload-based RDF graph fragmentation and allocation. In: EDBT, pp. 377–388 (2016)

11. Peng, P., Zou, L., Chen, L., Zhao, D.: Adaptive distributed RDF graph fragmentation and allocation based on query workload. IEEE Trans. Knowl. Data Eng. **31**(4), 670–685 (2019)
12. Peng, P., Zou, L., Guan, R.: Accelerating partial evaluation in distributed SPARQL query evaluation. In: ICDE, pp. 112–123 (2019)
13. Peng, P., Zou, L., Özsu, M.T., Chen, L., Zhao, D.: Processing SPARQL queries over distributed RDF graphs. VLDB J. **25**(2), 243–268 (2016)
14. Schätzle, A., Przyjaciel-Zablocki, M., Skilevic, S., Lausen, G.: S2RDF: RDF querying with SPARQL on spark. PVLDB **9**(10), 804–815 (2016)
15. Shao, B., Wang, H., Li, Y.: Trinity: a distributed graph engine on a memory cloud. In: SIGMOD, pp. 505–516 (2013)
16. Wu, B., Zhou, Y., Yuan, P., Liu, L., Jin, H.: Scalable SPARQL querying using path partitioning. In: ICDE, pp. 795–806 (2015)
17. Wylot, M., Mauroux, P.: DiploCloud: efficient and scalable management of RDF data in the cloud. TKDE, **PP**(99) (2015)

Classification-Based Emoji Recommendation for User Social Networks

Yuan Wang[1], Yukun Li[1,2(✉)], and Fenglian Liu[1,3]

[1] Tianjin University of Technology, 300384 Tianjin, China
www_wyuan@163.com, liyukun_tjut@163.com,
lflian@tjut.edu.cn
[2] Tianjin Key Laboratory of Intelligence Computing
and Novel Software Technology, Tianjin, China
[3] Key Laboratory of Computer Vision and System, Ministry of Education,
Tianjin, China

Abstract. Emoji recommendation focuses on solving time-consuming problem of finding emoji in social media platforms. The existing research works about emoji recommendation mainly take emoji as classification labels to train the relationship between emojis and texts by machine learning methods. However, they do not consider the one-to-many relationship between texts and emojis, nor do they pay attention to users' motivation to use emojis in real social media. At the same time, few studies make emoji recommendation based on Chinese corpus. This paper divides million-level Chinese micro-blog corpus into different context sets according to emojis, then propose a method to generate emoji-related features by analysis, finally a classification-based recommendation method is proposed by integrating these features. The experimental results show that the proposed method significantly improves the accuracy of emoji recommendation in social media platforms.

Keywords: Emoji-related feature · Classification · Emoji recommendation

1 Introduction

Multiple forms of visual expression, including emoticons, emojis, stickers, and memes, have become prevalent along the development of the Internet, gradually changing people's narrative structure. Especially, emojis are being adopted at a faster rate than any other "language" and most of us now use the colorful symbols to communicate. But only limited emojis can be displayed on a very small screen of cellphone. With the increasing of the variety and quantity of visual expression, users always have to open visual expression folder and scroll up and down to choose the most suitable one from hundreds of different emoji icons, which seriously affects the experience of people and also increases the search time of user. Therefore, it becomes an interesting research issues that how to automatically recommend suitable emojis to users according to the contexts.

In order to solve this problem, researchers put forward emoji prediction methods by exploring the relationship between texts and emojis. However there still exist some

© Springer Nature Switzerland AG 2019
J. Song and X. Zhu (Eds.): APWeb-WAIM 2019 Workshops, LNCS 11809, pp. 8–22, 2019.
https://doi.org/10.1007/978-3-030-33982-1_2

problems that causing recommendation results inaccurate. The deeper cause is failure to focus on users' motivation to use emojis in real social media. First of all, people tend to use emojis on social media with text in order to express their emotions or reveal meanings hidden by figurative language. Secondly, emoji cannot be used as the sole marker of the context, and the same context may be suitable for adding different emojis. For example, you send a short message to a friend: "I fell and hit my head on the cupboard". Your friends probably do not know whether to sympathize with you or laugh at you. If you add a "sad" emoji at the end of this sentence, it is equivalent to providing a non-verbal clue, "I feel very painful". If you add a "tear in laughter" emoji at the end, it means a little self-mockery. What's more, there is no relevant work focusing on the cross-cutting between the use of emojis and its cultural background. For example, there are some hot words (like "开森") which should be correctly explained in Chinese context. Another key reason is the incomplete feature extraction of word vectors, because the limitation of corpus.

This problem meets some challenges. At first, the understanding to the semantic relationship between texts and emojis is a challenging task because emojis often have different interpretations that depend on the reader. Second, the imbalance of the emoji data set used in social context, because there are some emojis are often used, while others are rarely used.

This paper studied the problem and proposed a solution. The main contributions can be summarized as follows:

(1) A method of constructing emoji-related features is proposed. Specifically, it includes emoji-related context document representation, constructing emoji-related keywords dictionary, and constructing relevance features of emojis.
(2) A method of emoji recommendation by integrating emoji-related features is proposed, as well as the method of classifying emojis based on emotions also is defined.
(3) The emoji usage data set is established and the proposed method is evaluated based on the data set. By designing a special micro-blog specialized crawler, 5 million data of Weibo are collected. Based on this data set, the validity of the proposed method is verified.

2 Related Work

Emoji prediction is an emerging problem [1], which combines the nuances of emotional analysis and the noisy data features of social media. The current research work mainly focuses on single text feature based emoji prediction and multi-feature fusion based emoji prediction.

The research based on single text feature mainly focuses on context representation and semantic analysis of context. Effrosynidis et al. [2] used TF-IDF vector context combined with linear SVC classification algorithm, using word tri-grams to train prediction model. Chen et al. [3] proposed a method based on vector similarity to generate a vector for tweet, and then used cosine similarity method to find the most appropriate emoji symbols. Çöltekin and Rama [4] proposed using n-gram to represent text features and using linear classification model SVM to capture local dependencies to achieve emoji prediction, and the result is better than RNN. Wang and Pedersen [5] realized multi-channel CNN network model to predict Emoji by improving word embedding method. As the constant development and Improvement of natural language information processing, more attention has been paid to the use of semantic analysis techniques to analyze text. Barbieri et al. [1] proposed a semantic model of emojis based on LSTM neural network, and explored the relationship between words and emoji. Xie et al. [6] encoded the context information in the dialogue using a hierarchical LSTM network, and then predicted it according to the dialog representation they learned. Wu et al. [7] proposed a method to representation tweets through combining CNN and LSTM layers.

The research based on multi-feature fusion mainly considers fusion text features, emotional features, external environment features and so on. Guibon et al. [8] proposed a multi-label stochastic forest algorithm model which combines text features and emotion-related features to predict emoji. Choudhary et al. [9] constructed an emotional classification tool, using emoji as a tag for emotional analysis, to further predict emoji without emoji data. Baziotis et al. [10] used Bi-LSTM with attention and pre-trained word2vec vectors to predict emoji by using external resources to link each tweet with emotional, specific and familiarity information. Liu [11] put forward two models to improve the classification of multiple emoji by utilizing general text features and adding some external resources such as various artificial dictionaries of affective words.

Emoji can smooth online communication, particularly when tones such as sarcasm and dry wit are difficult to display in text-based communication [12]. In fact, individuals can incorporate playful elements into the more mundane message by adding different emoji [13, 14]. For instance, Zhou et al. [15] reported that their participants would add an emoji if they believed that their text might cause negative feelings on the receiving end.

The above research work focuses on how to effectively extract emoji-related text features to represent the relationship between emojis and texts from the perspective of text. In fact, every emoji has its corresponding semantic representation. In this paper, emoji is labeled by the way of "[ ]". For example, 😨 corresponds to "[sad]" in the text. The word "sad" and its related words are very important for understanding the relationship between texts and emojis. Our main contribution in this paper is to effectively represent the relationship between emojis and texts from the perspective of emoji. At the same time, most emojis have obvious emotional tendencies and people also tend to use emoji's emotional characteristics to express their emotions or attitudes for one people or one thing. Our work focuses on recommendation several emojis for a sentence, because users may express different emotions for one sentence with different emojis. Based on above reasons, we first propose extracting emoji-related features, including emoji-related keywords feature, each emoji context document feature representation, relevance features of emojis. Next we propose a method to compute similarity score for every sentence with different emojis. Finally, several emojis with high similarity are used as recommended results.

3   Constructing Emoji-Related Features

This section introduces the whole process of constructing emoji-related features. Section 3.1 proposes constructing emoji-related context document set based on the multi-context features of emoji. Section 3.2 describes how to represent context features of each emoji. Section 3.3 describes how to construct and expand the emoji-related keywords dictionary. In Sect. 3.4, the relevance of emojis is quantified based on millions of corpus.

3.1   Emoji-Related Context Document Definition and Preprocessing

Since its birth, emoji has undergone tremendous changes in form, and its connotation and functions are also more abundant. Because emoji and language interact semantically, we can have a deeper understanding of the unique usage rules of each emoji through analyzing each emoji's context. Therefore, this paper proposes to construct emoji-related context document based on the multi-context features of each emoji. We first introduce some notations in this paper. Let $E = \{e_1, e_2, \ldots, e_n\}$ denotes the overall emoji sets, where n is taken as the number of emoji. Let $C = \{c_1, c_2, \ldots, c_n\}$ denotes the all emoji context corpus, and let $c_i = \{s_{i1}, s_{i2}, \ldots, s_{im}\}$ denotes all context corpus of e_i, s_{i1} is explained the first context with e_i. For instance, 😭 as emoji label, its context document is consists of many emoji-related sentences, such as, $s_1 = \{$I had already arrived at the subway station before I realized that there was no subway card with me.$\}$, $s_2 = \{$I failed my interview today.$\}$, etc.

The original corpus is divided into several emoji-related documents according to the above definition, which are called emoji-related target documents. Next, preprocess all target documents returned from the segmentation processing, including denoising, word segmentation and deletion of stop words. Considering there are some network hot words and popular language in our corpus, we set up a custom dictionary during the process of word segmentation in order to ensure these words will not be separated. Table 1 shows some words and interpretation of word meaning in a custom dictionary. Finally, all word segmentation results of each emoji-related target document are generated.

Table 1. Some words of customized dictionary

ID	Hot words	Meaning
1	脑残	Brain dead
2	真无语	Speechless
3	好桑心	Sad/Hurt
4	装嫩	Pretend to be young
5	窝火	Choke with resentment

3.2   Emoji-Related Context Document Representation

This section introduces how to represent different documents in a unified way so as to distinguish the usage of emoji. At first, word segmentation results of all target documents are used to establish a public dictionary. Second, we use bag of words model to represent each target document. Third, we use TF-IDF algorithm to add the weight to keyword. Finally, the eigenvector of emoji-related context document are generated.

First of all, we construct a lexicon based on word segmentation results of all target documents and get the order of words. Next, we use word model to represent features of every target document. The main idea is to use the target list data as the bag-of-word data, then number all words in the bag with numbers, and get the corresponding relationship between numbers and words. And then, each target document is represented as a set of vectors through bag of word model, the elements in the vector are a two-tuple (number, term frequency), corresponding to each word in the document after word segmentation. And next, consider that some words are representative, as well as the main idea of TF-IDF [16] is that if a word or phrase appears frequently in an article and rarely in other articles, it is considered that the word or phrase has good classification ability and is suitable for classification. Therefore, bag of words representation of each document is transformed into TF-IDF representation by TF-IDF weighting strategy. The TF-IDF value of each word in each document is obtained.

TF-IDF is a classical statistical method for calculating the weight of words, which is composed of term frequency (TF) and inverse document frequency (IDF). The word frequency calculation is shown in formula (1).

$$tf_{i,j} = \frac{n_{i,j}}{\sum_k n_{k,j}} \tag{1}$$

$tf_{i,j}$ represents the frequently of w_i, $n_{i,j}$ represents the number of w_i in j emoji-related document. $\sum_k n_{k,j}$ represents the sum of the number of occurrences of k words in j document. The inverse document frequency calculation is shown in formula (2).

$$idf_j = log \frac{|D|}{1 + |\{j : t_i \in d_i\}|} \tag{2}$$

IDF is a measure of the universal importance of a word. Where: $|D|$ represents the total number of all documents. $|\{j : t_i \in d_i\}|$ denotes the number of documents containing the word t_i. Finally, the calculation of the normalization of TF-ID is shown in formula (3).

$$tfidf_{i,j} = tf_{i,j} \times idf_j \tag{3}$$

Finally, we gain the TF-IDF values for each word in each target document, as well as the eigenvector of each emoji-related target document is also generated.

3.3   Constructing Emoji-Related KeyWords Dictionary

Propose 2 methods of constructing feature word [17] lexicon highly related to emoji in this section, one is to extract keywords based emoji-related corpus through the word vector model, the other is to construct emoji-related sentiment words based on existing sentiment lexicon. Finally, a new representative emoji keyword dictionary is obtained by merging the feature words obtained in two ways.

The first method is described below. First of all, due to every emoji has its corresponding semantic representation, so every emojis' semantic word is used as target feature word for this emoji. Next, we using a large scale emoji-related data set to train word model and through the calculation of similarity to add associated words with the emoji target feature words into the lexicon and regard these associated words as target word to iteratively compute similarity. Finally, all words are in every emoji's lexicon.

The Word2vec is one of the word vector models. It can map all words in the corpus into a short vector with fixed length, and all the vectors form a word vector space. So each word is equivalent to a point in the space, the similarity between words can be judged by the "distance" between points in the space. The CBOW and the Skip-Gram is main model of Word2vec. They are shown in Fig. 1.

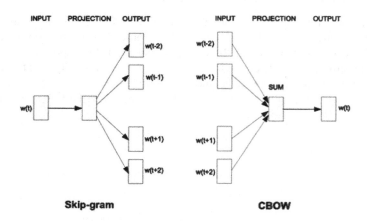

Fig. 1. Skip-gram model and CBOW model of Word2vec

The Skip-Gram model predicts the context $S_{w(t)} = (w_{(t-k)}, \ldots, w_{(t-1)}, w_{(t)}, w_{(t+1)}, \ldots, w_{(t + k)})$ by inputting word $w_{(t)}$, K is the size of the context window of $w_{(t)}$, that is the number of selected words in left and in right. The CBOW model is contrary to Skip-Gram model, it predict $w_{(t)}$ through context $S_{w(t)}$.

We use gensim of python to implement Word2Vec. In order to train model, the model input is processed 250,000 emoji-related corpus. Corresponding semantic words of emojis are used as target feature, the model outputs the related words with target feature through calculating the similarity between the feature words and others words of corpus.

The second method is described as below. We first merge the existing sentiment dictionaries, then delete the repetitive words, and finally get a new sentiment dictionary. We travel word segmentation results of each emoji-related target document to match new sentiment dictionary, we gain each emoji-related sentiment lexicon finally.

A new representative emoji keyword dictionary is obtained by merging the feature words obtained in two ways. The final result of construction for "[Disappointment]' and "[be shocked]" are shown in the Table 2.

Table 2. The words describing a feature

Feature	words
[Disappointment]	低落 堕落 悲伤 失望 难受 衰 没意思 负能量 哎 心伤 逞强 事与愿违 事故 可怜 争吵
[be shocked]	居然 竟然 吃惊 震惊 夸张 壮观 厉害 奇迹 强大 怎么 严重 神奇 意外 叹为观止 吓一跳

3.4   Constructing Relevance Feature of Emojis

Considering the multi-contextual features of emoji in real social situation, this section proposes to construct emoji classification model in order to cluster emoji with similar contextual usage. The key idea of the model proposed in this paper is to first representation emoji-related context document, then calculate similarity, next define this feature as similarity features between emojis, and finally use k-means to cluster emoji. The specific steps of emoji classification model are shown in the following Fig. 2.

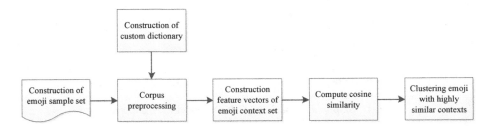

Fig. 2. Emoji classification model

We can gain each emoji document context representation with the methods of the Sect. 3.2. In this section, the cosine similarity between each emoji context set and all emoji context set is calculated by cycling each emoji context set, and n multi-dimensional feature vectors are obtained. The larger value in the vector, the more similar context two emoji within, which means two emoji are closer. Formula (4) shows the cosine similarity calculation between documents.

$$\cos\theta = \frac{\sum_{i=1}^{n}(a_i \times b_i)}{\sqrt{\sum_{i=1}^{n}(a_i)^2} \times \sqrt{\sum_{i=1}^{n}(b_i)^2}} = \frac{A \cdot B}{|A| \times |B|} \qquad (4)$$

A represents the feature vector of one emoji document, a_i represents ith element in vector A. B represents the feature vector of another emoji document, b_i represents ith element in vector B. $A \cdot B$ represents the dot product of the two vectors. $|A| \cdot |B|$ represents the product of absolute values of two vectors. And the specific algorithm is shown in Algorithm 1.

Algorithm 1. Similarity Computation Based on Emoji-Related Document Context Representation

---

Input: Feature vector of each document $\{A_1, A_2, A_3, ..., A_n\}$
Output: Similarity matrix R_{n*n}, each row in matrix is an n-dimensional vector representing relevance feature of emojis.
1. **For** i from 1 to n **do**
2.   **For** j from 1 to n **do**
3. $r_{ij} = \cos\theta = \frac{A_i \cdot A_j}{|A_i| \times |A_j|}$
4.   **End for**
5. **End for**
6. **Return** R_{n*n}

Through the calculation, the similar weight vectors of each emoji and other emojis are obtained. The similar weight vectors of each emoji can be mapped to a point in high latitude space. The omni-directional N-dimension of the vector measures the use of context-based expressions. K-Means algorithm is an unsupervised clustering algorithm. It is relatively simple to implement and has good clustering effect. So we choose it to cluster emoji. Finally, emojis are divided into several categories.

4 Integrated Recommendation Method

Three emoji-related features have obtained in Sect. 3. Given three features: emoji-related context document representation, emoji-related keywords dictionary, the correlations features between of emojis. Next, we propose the recommendation method by integrating them. The details of our method are shown as follows.

4.1 Recommendation Method by Integrating Emoji-Related Features

The key idea of the algorithm proposed in this paper is: For a given sentence by user input, segmentation words for this sentence first. On the one hand, the results of word segmentation are used to match emoji-related keywords dictionaries and get the number of feature words in each emoji-related dictionary, and each feature number represents the correlation between the input text and one emoji. In order to calculate the similarity between input text and different emojis, we sum each emoji-related feature number as the total feature number, and then use the quotient between the feature numbers of each emoji and the total feature number to represent the similarity. On the other hand, the results of word segmentation are used for text representation according Sect. 3.2, and then utilize cosine similarity of the vector to calculate the similarity between test document and each target document, and each value in the vector represents the similarity between the test document and each emoji. Finally, we add up the two similarity values to get a new value, which is used as the final recommendation result.

All emojis are divided into categories by calculating the correlations features between emojis, which category represents the similarity of emoji usage. We find that the classification result tends to classify emoji emotions, and it is highly relevant to the user's motivation to use it. We ask five experts to fine-tune the classification results to ensure the accuracy of the classification results. Finally, the classification results are used to expand the emoji verification set, the aim is to classification emotions of emojis.

4.2   Recommendation Generation

The new similarity results vector is taken as the basis of the recommendation at first, and then we use the bubble sorting algorithm to sort similarity values from high to low. Finally, we recommend several emojis with high similarity to the test document as recommend result. The detailed process of ranking-based emoji recommendation is shown in Algorithm 2.

Algorithm 2. Ranking-Based Emoji Recommendation

```
Input: Similarity vectors R, threshold N
Output: The top N emoji label in the sorted array.
1.  For i from 0 to length-1
2.     For j from 0 to length-1-i
3.        If (array[j] > array[j+1])
4.           Swap(array[j], array[j+1])
5.        End if
6.     End for
7.  End for
8.  For k from 0 to N-1
9.     array[k]->label[k]
10. End for
11. Return label
```

---

5 Experiment Results and Analysis

This section mainly introduces how to design experiments and proves the effectiveness of the proposed method. Section 5.1 introduces the work of data acquisition and cleaning. Section 5.2 introduces the processing of extracting emojis and dividing the experimental dataset. Section 5.3 defines the evaluation indicators of experiments result. And the last section analyses the experimental results.

5.1 Data Acquisition and Cleaning

Considering that few studies focuses on emoji prediction based on Chinese text, and there is no open data set. Therefore, this paper chooses to use data acquisition tool octopus collector for data acquisition. Nearly 50,000 microblog data of 2000 users are collected as standby corpus. The preliminary collected Weibo data contain a large amount of noise and redundant data, so it is necessary to pre-process the data to generate a basic corpus. After a series of data cleaning operations, a fixed format of the corpus are obtained, with only one emoji at the end of a sentence. The key operations of pretreatment include filtering out non-emoji text, deleting microblogs with multiple emojis, deleting hyperlinks, @ User name, #Topic Name#, \\ Forwarding content.

5.2 Extraction of Emojis and Setting up Experimental Data Set

In the micro-blog text, each emoji has corresponding Chinese meanings, marked with "[]", such as 😊 corresponding to [[亲亲]]. After data cleaning in Sect. 5.1, 150,000 microblog sentences with one emoji are obtained, and 163 emoji are counted. Considering that little emoji corpus is not enough to express the contextual usage characteristics of the emoji, we filtered out emoji corpus with less than 1000 microblog sentences. Finally, 47 kinds of emoji are obtained, and the total number of emoji reaches 100,000. The extracted emoji are displayed in the Table 3.

Table 3. Emoji set screened from data sets

Emoji

Table 4. Statistics of the dataset

Dataset	#Emoji	#Train	#Test
Weibo	47	98586	940

In order to balance the test corpus, we cycle each emoji label and randomly select 20 contexts of each emoji to form a test set containing 940 contexts. The statistics of dataset are listed in Table 4.

5.3   Evaluating Indicator

This section mainly uses the accuracy to analyze the experimental results. Generally speaking, the higher the accuracy, the more effective the proposed method is. The recommended accuracy calculation method is shown in formula (5).

$$\text{Accuracy} = \frac{n}{N} \tag{5}$$

N is used to represent the total number of test sets and n is used to represent the number of correct recommendations. For the definition of n, considering that emoji classification is based on the contextual similarity of emoji, so emoji belonging to the same category are very similar in the context usage. Therefore, we use emoji classification results to expand the emoji verification set, as long as one of the recommended results is included in the emoji verification set. We define the recommendation is correct.

5.4   Experimental Analysis

Firstly, 47 emojis are divided into different categories, and then we choose the optimal number of categories as our experimental category settings, and final the classification results are fine-tuned by five experts. We define D as average distance within a class divided by average distance between classes. K is defined as the number of categories classified by emoji. Different K values have different D, the smaller the D value, the greater the degree of aggregation within a class and the smaller the degree of separation between classes, the better the classification effect. But considering the actual situation, K can't be chosen too large. The relationship between K and D is shown in the Fig. 3.

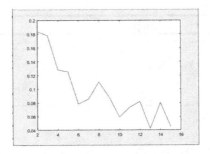

Fig. 3. The relationship between K and D

Based on the above analysis, we find that D is the smallest when K = 6, 10, 13, but consider that there are 47 emojis categories, when K = 13, it accounts for more than 1/3 of the number of categories to remove this point. Next, we test K = 6 and 10, and compare which classification is better. The following tables present the results of emoji classification when K = 6 and K = 10.

Secondly, we set the scope of N according to the actual needs of users. For the selection of recommendation threshold, we surveyed 30 emoji users. More than half of users mentioned that they use emoji more often every day and spend more than 10 s on finding emoji on average. They stress that if can narrow downed the emoji choices, they might save a few minutes or even longer to do something more valuable every day. At the same time, ninety percent of them believed that the number of recommended emoji should be between 3 and 5. They believed that too many recommendation results would increase their operate burden, and too few recommendation results might be less efficient than users' search efficiency. Therefore, this paper select 3, 4 and 5 recommendation numbers as experimental thresholds, and finally determines the most effective recommendation number according to the accuracy of the recommendation (Tables 5 and 6).

Table 5. All emojis are classified into six categories

Type	Emoji
1	
2	
3	
4	
5	
6	

For each emoji in the experiment, we randomly select 20 contexts to compose our test set. Verifying recommendation method by using test sets, we come to the conclusion as show in the figure below. Figure 4 shows the trend of correct recommendation for each emoji under different combinations of emoji classification and recommendation thresholds. The abscissa represents the each emoji and the ordinate represents the number of correct recommendation in 20 contexts. We can see that there are some emojis with low accuracy in Fig. 4. We analyze the possible reasons as follows. The first is the number of corpus may limit the extraction of emoji usage features, resulting in inaccurate recommendation. The second is that some emojis are used flexibly in real context. These emojis (like 😊) often appear in various contexts, which make it difficult to extract emoji usage features.

Table 6. All emojis are classified into ten categories

Type	Emoji
1	
2	
3	
4	
5	
6	
7	
8	
9	
10	

At the same time, we also set up four comparative experiments in order to prove the effectiveness of our proposed method. The difference between the four groups of experiments is that the added features are different, and the calculation method of these features is the same as the method proposed in this paper. The last group of experiments represents the proposed method, and the bold numbers in the table represent the accuracy of the proposed method. We use the combination of TF-IDF and Doc2bow (mainly used to implement Bow model based on document) to obtain emoji-related context features.

The specific experimental accuracy is shown in the Table 7 below. We can see that the accuracy is higher when the number of classification categories K = 6. The accuracy of recommendation is higher when emoji-related feature words are added separately. The proposed method in this paper combines the characteristics of the above two baselines, and we can see that the accuracy of this method is the highest in the four experiments.

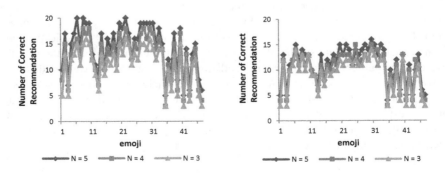

Fig. 4. Detailed recommendation results under different N thresholds when K = 6 and K = 10

Table 7. Accuracy for different baseline when N = 6 and N = 10

Experience settings	Accuracy (K = 5)	
	N = 6	N = 10
Doc2bow+TF-IDF	0.667	0.543
Doc2bow+TF-IDF+Emoji-related sentiment keywords	0.679	0.557
Doc2bow+TF-IDF+Emoji-related keywords	0.695	0.555
Doc2bow+TF-IDF+Fusing emoji-related keywords	**0.722**	**0.563**

6 Conclusion

In this paper, we propose the construction method of emoji-related features, including emoji-related context document representation, constructing emoji-related keywords dictionary, and constructing relevance feature between of emojis. Next we propose a similarity calculation method for each feature, and then getting a new vector of emoji-related similarity values by integrating each similarity feature. Finally, we sort similarity values from high to low and recommend several emojis with high similarity to the test document as recommend result. The results of the experiment prove the effectiveness of recommendation method based on emoji classification.

Acknowledgement. This research was supported by the Natural Science Foundation of Tianjin (No. 15JCYBJC46500), the Training plan of Tianjin University Innovation Team (No. TD13-5025), and the Major Project of Tianjin Smart Manufacturing (No. 15ZXZN CX00050).

References

1. Barbieri, F., Ballesteros, M., Saggion, H.: Are emojis predictable? In: Proceedings of the 15th Conference of the European Chapter of the Association for Computational Linguistics: Volume 2, Short Papers, pp. 105–111 (2017)
2. Effrosynidis, D.: DUTH at SemEval-2018 Task 2: emoji prediction in tweets. In: Proceedings of the 12th International Workshop on Semantic Evaluation, SemEval@NAACL-HLT, New Orleans, Louisiana, USA, 5–6 June 2018, pp. 466–469 (2018)
3. Chen, J., Yang, D., Li, X., Chen, W., Wang, T.: Peperomia at SemEval-2018 Task 2 : vector similarity based approach for emoji prediction. In: Proceedings of the 12th International Workshop on Semantic Evaluation, SemEval@NAACL-HLT, New Orleans, Louisiana, USA, 5–6 June 2018, pp. 428–432 (2018)
4. Rama, T.: Tübingen-Oslo at SemEval-2018 Task 2 : SVMs perform better than RNNs at emoji prediction. In: Proceedings of the 12th International Workshop on Semantic Evaluation, SemEval@NAACL-HLT, New Orleans, Louisiana, USA, 5–6 June 2018, pp. 34–38 (2018)
5. Wang, Z., Pedersen, T.: UMDSub at SemEval-2018 Task 2 : multilingual emoji prediction multi-channel convolutional neural network on subword embedding. In: Proceedings of the 12th International Workshop on Semantic Evaluation, SemEval@NAACL-HLT, New Orleans, Louisiana, USA, 5–6 June 2018, pp. 395–399 (2018)

6. Xie, R., Liu, Z., Yan, R., Sun, M.: Neural emoji recommendation in dialogue systems. arXiv e-prints (2016). http://arxiv.org/abs/1612.04609
7. Wu, C., Wu, F., Wu, S., Yuan, Z.: THU NGN at SemEval-2018 Task 2 : residual CNN-LSTM network with attention for English emoji prediction. In: Proceedings of the 12th International Workshop on Semantic Evaluation, SemEval@NAACL-HLT, New Orleans, Louisiana, USA, 5–6 June 2018, pp. 410–414 (2018)
8. Guibon, G., Ochs, M., Bellot, P.: Prédiction automatique d' emojis sentimentaux. In: The 14th French Information Retrieval Conference, Marseille, France, 29–31 March 2017, pp. 59–74 (2017)
9. Choudhary, N., Singh, R., Rao, V.A., Shrivastava, M.: Twitter corpus of resource-scarce languages for sentiment analysis and multilingual emoji prediction. In: Proceedings of the 27th International Conference on Computational Linguistics, COLING, Santa Fe, New Mexico, USA, 20–26 August 2018, pp. 1570–1577 (2018). http://www.aclweb.org/anthology/C18-1133
10. Baziotis, C., Athanasiou, N., Paraskevopoulos, G., Ellinas, N., Kolovou, A., Potamianos, A.: NTUA-SLP at SemEval-2018 Task 2 : predicting emojis using RNNs with context-aware attention. In: Proceedings of the 12th International Workshop on Semantic Evaluation, SemEval@NAACL-HLT, New Orleans, Louisiana, USA, 5–6 June 2018, pp. 438–444 (2018)
11. Liu, Man.: EmoNLP at SemEval-2018 Task 2 : english emoji prediction with gradient boosting regression tree method and bidirectional LSTM. In: Proceedings of the 12th International Workshop on Semantic Evaluation, SemEval@NAACL-HLT, New Orleans, Louisiana, USA, 5–6 June 2018, pp. 390–394 (2018)
12. Kaye, L.K., Wall, H.J., Malone, S.A.: "Turn that frown upside-down": a contextual account of emoticon usage on different virtual platforms. Comput. Hum. Behav. **60**, 463–467 (2016). https://doi.org/10.1016/j.chb.2016.02.088
13. Hu, T., Guo, H., Sun, H., Nguyen, T.V.T., Luo, J.: Spice up your chat: the intentions and sentiment effects of using emojis. In: Proceedings of the Eleventh International Conference on Web and Social Media, ICWSM, Canada, 15–18 May 2017, pp. 102–111 (2017). http://arxiv.org/abs/1703.02860
14. Ma, X.: From internet memes to emoticon engineering: insights from the baozou comic phenomenon in China. In: Human-Computer Interaction. Novel User Experiences - 18th International Conference, HCI International, Toronto, ON, Canada, 17–22 July 2016, pp. 15–27 (2016). https://doi.org/10.1007/978-3-319-39513-5
15. Zhou, R., Hentschel, J., Kumar, N.: Goodbye text, hello emoji : mobile communication on WeChat in China. In: Proceedings of the 2017 CHI Conference on Human Factors in Computing Systems, Denver, CO, USA, 06–11 May 2017, pp. 748–759 (2017)
16. Salton, G., Yu, C.T.: On the construction of effective vocabularies for information retrieval. In: Proceedings of the 1973 meeting on Programming Languages and Information Retrieval, Gaithersburg, Maryland, USA, 4–6 November 1973, pp. 48–60 (1973)
17. Wu, Y., Li, Y., Hao, G.: A web-based theme-related word set construction algorithm. In: Web and Big Data - APWeb-WAIM 2018 International Workshops: MWDA, BAH, KGMA, DMMOOC, DS, Macau, China, 23–25 July 2018, pp. 188-200 (2018)

Leveraging Context Information for Joint Entity and Relation Linking

Yao Zhao[1], Zhuoming Xu[1(✉)], and Wei Hu[2]

[1] College of Computer and Information,
Hohai University, Nanjing 210098, China
{vodka, zmxu}@hhu.edu.cn
[2] State Key Laboratory for Novel Software Technology,
Nanjing University, Nanjing 210023, China
whu@nju.edu.cn

Abstract. As an important module in most knowledge base question answering (KBQA) systems, entity and relation linking maps proper nouns and relational phrases to corresponding semantic constructs (entities and relations, respectively) in a given KB. Because different entities/relations may have the same mentions, joint disambiguation has been proposed to identify the exact entity/relation from a list of candidates using context information. Existing joint disambiguation methods, like the method in EARL (Entity and Relation Linker), mainly focus on modeling the co-occurrence probabilities of different entities and relations in input questions, while paying little attention to other non-mention expressions (e.g., wh-words). In this paper, we propose the Extended Entity and Relation Linker (EEARL), which leverages full context information to improve linking accuracy. EEARL firstly extracts the context information for each mention and the attribute features for each entity/relation via character-level and word-level LSTMs and constructs context vectors and feature vectors, respectively, and then calculates the similarity between the two vectors to re-score all the candidates. Experimental results on two benchmark datasets (LC-QuAD and QALD) show that EEARL outperforms EARL and several baseline methods in terms of both entity linking and relation linking accuracy.

Keywords: Entity linking · Relation linking · Joint entity and relation linking · knowledge base question answering · Context information

1 Introduction

knowledge base question answering (KBQA) systems transform natural language questions to executable queries (e.g., SPARQL queries) over KBs [1]. Entity and relation linking is an important module in most KBQA systems, which maps proper nouns and relational phrases (i.e., keyword phrases) to entities and relations (or relation chains), respectively, in a given KB. One main difficulty in this linking step is that, the entities and relations contained in natural language questions are often inconsistent with their representations in the KB, which means that mapping the entities and relations in natural language questions to the KB based solely upon the spelling of the words does not work very well. Therefore, how to accurately link the entities and

J. Song and X. Zhu (Eds.): APWeb-WAIM 2019 Workshops, LNCS 11809, pp. 23–36, 2019.
https://doi.org/10.1007/978-3-030-33982-1_3

relations to the correct ones in the KB is especially important. In most entity linking systems like [2], entity/relation disambiguation is typically performed by calculating the co-occurrence probability with other entities and relations in an input question. However, when the length of the input question is short, it is often unable to get enough information from the mentions in the context. Therefore, it will be more efficient to combine the input entities and relations to optimize the disambiguation.

To this end, Dubey et al. [3] proposed a method for joint disambiguation of entities and relations, called EARL (Entity and Relation Linker). Specifically, EARL uses statistical ideas to calculate the number of relations around each entity, and this number is then used as a feature to train the model used to generate matching scores for candidate elements. The candidate element with the highest score is considered as the best candidate. Meanwhile, the method formalizes the joint entity and relation linking task into the Generalized Traveling Salesman Problem (GTSP) [4], and thus this NP-hard problem can be approximately solved in polynomial time.

EARL regards entities and relations as nodes and edges in a graph, and effectively utilizes the graph structure information. However, this method also has a few limitations. For example, the non-entity/non-relation vocabularies in the context are not exploited. Let us consider the following example: "Where was the father of Barack Obama born?" According to EARL, all non-entity/non-relation words would be discarded. Thus, it only recognizes "Barack Obama" as an entity and "born" as a relation, and generates candidate elements for them separately. Similarly, for the question "When was the father of Barack Obama born?", it would produce the same result as the previous question. However, the two questions are about location ("where") and time ("when"), respectively, so the answers to them are obviously different. EARL is therefore ineffective in terms of relation disambiguation.

In view of the shortcomings of EARL, we propose an improved entity and relation joint linking method, called EEARL (Extended Entity and Relation Linker). The basic idea of EEARL is that, when dealing with relation linking, we consider not only the impact of entities and relations in the context, but also the impact of other non-entity/non-relation vocabularies (e.g., wh-words). More specifically, when a candidate element is generated for a relation, we extract the domain, range, type, and the local name of the relation URI, and merge them into the feature vector. Meanwhile, we use the Long Short-Term Memory (LSTM) [5] network to fuse the important non-entity/non-relation vocabularies in the context into the context vector, and calculate the similarity between the two vectors as the final score.

We conducted performance evaluation experiments on two typical benchmark datasets, LC-QuAD [6] and QALD-7 [7], to compare EEARL with EARL and several baseline methods. The experimental results show that EEARL outperforms EARL and the baseline methods in terms of both entity linking and relation linking accuracy.

In summary, the main contributions of this paper are listed as follows:

- We propose to leverage full context information for entity and relation linking.
- We use a word-level LSTM to capture non-entity/non-relation information in the context, a character-level LSTM to complete the domain/range vector and a word-level LSTM to represent the relation URI's local name for feature modeling.

- We integrate our extensions into EARL, thereby forming EEARL and achieving performance improvement in terms of entity/relation linking accuracy.

The remainder of this paper is organized as follows. Section 2 briefly reviews the work related to entity and relation linking. On the basis of the idea of EARL, we describe our improved method EEARL in Sect. 3. Section 4 reports the experimental results of performance evaluation. Finally, we conclude this paper and discuss future work in Sect. 5.

2 Related Work

Entity and relation linking has attracted many researchers' attention. Ratinov et al. [8] first used a local optimization scheme to link each entity phrase for obtaining a sub-optimal solution with certain quality, and then calculated the association characteristics between the candidate entity and other entities according to the suboptimal solution, which was finally used to train the entire model. The S-MART model was proposed by Yang and Chang [9], which resolves the limitation that multiple entity phrases cannot overlap. In this method, all phrases are linked by the Forward-Backward algorithm to ensure that, when the phrases overlap, at most one phrase points to a specific entity, and the rest points to an empty entity. AGDISTIS [10] is a graph-based disambiguation system based on the hop count distance between candidate objects for multiple entities in a given text.

Due to its particularity, relation mapping generally needs to be analyzed for specific situations. The word embedding model tackles the semantic heterogeneity in relation mapping by learning a plausible vector representation for each word from a large amount of corpus. Many models, e.g., ReMatch [11] and RelMatch [12], use WordNet [13] similarity for relation mapping, and have achieved promising results.

Many existing KBQA systems employ a generic entity linking tool for entity linking. Most of them are based on the context or other entities in the same sentence to disambiguate. However, in practice, a question may contain few entities, which makes it ineffective to disambiguate based on other entities. To overcome this limitation, many KBQA systems have recently been developed. For example, Dubey et al. [3] firstly linked entities, and then generated candidate relation linking based on the result of entity linking, and finally selected the best candidate relations through for example semantic similarity techniques. In this method, the relation mapping depends on the entity linking. If the entity linking goes wrong, the error would be transmitted and amplified. In other systems like XSER [14], entity linking and relation mapping are executed independently.

Compared with the above existing methods, our proposed method combines entity linking and relation linking together, which not only solves the problem of lack of information caused by considering entity linking and relation linking separately, but also alleviates the problem of error amplification caused by backward propagation. Additionally, it considers non-entity/non-relation vocabulary information in the context to improve linking accuracy.

3   EEARL: Extended Entity and Relation Linker

Given a KB, existing entity and relation linking methods usually identify the boundaries of words first, and then use the information of other entities/relations to generate a
list of candidate elements and disambiguate them. For the task of joint disambiguation,
the entities and relations are collectively considered when generating candidate elements, and more reliable candidate elements are generated based on the information of
entities and relations. The EEARL method proposed in this paper uses (1) the SENNA
tool [15] to extract keyword phrases from the input natural language questions, (2) the
character-level LSTM [5] to predict the entity/relation types of keyword phrases,
(3) ElasticSearch [16] to generate candidate element lists, and calculates scores based
on the connection density and context information to obtain the best entity/relation
mappings in the KB. The detailed processing flow chart for the EEARL method is
illustrated in Fig. 1, where the context information score computation is our main
contribution.

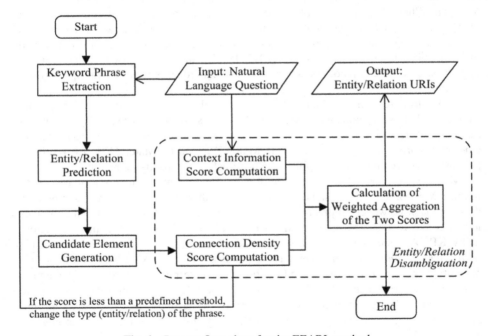

Fig. 1. Process flow chart for the EEARL method

3.1   Keyword Phrase Extraction

Given a natural language question, first we need to extract the words that represent
entities and relations. We select SENNA [15] as our keyword phrase extraction tool,
which uses word vectors for natural language processing tasks such as named entity

recognition and part-of-speech (POS) tagging. Additionally, we prepare a list of stop words for eliminating the impact of non-entity/non-relation words on the word segmentation results. For instance, given a question "When was the father of Barack Obama born?", we extract three keyword phrases: "father", "Barack Obama", and "born".

3.2 Entity/Relation Prediction

After the keyword phrases are extracted, the next step is to predict their entity/relation types, so as to adopt different processing strategies. For this prediction task, character-level models can better handle out-of-vocabulary (OOV) words [17], so we employ a character-level LSTM. In this paper, we follow the original EARL [3] to train the prediction model. More specifically, as in [3], we use the "multi-task learning method with hard parameter sharing" to improve the generalization ability of the method and reduce the parameter size. The loss function is defined by Eq. (1) [3]:

$$\zeta = (1 - \alpha) \times \zeta_{BCE} + \alpha \times \zeta_{ED} \tag{1}$$

where ζ_{BCE} denotes the binary cross-entropy loss of the learning target as a phrase of an entity or relation, and ζ_{ED} denotes the square of the Euclidean distance between the predicted embedding and the correct embedding of the tag. We empirically select α as 0.25.

For the keyword phrases extracted from the previous question, the LSTM network predicts "father" and "born" as two relations and "Barack Obama" as an entity.

3.3 Candidate Element Generation

After extracting the word representation of an entity/relation, we need to generate a list of candidate elements for it and find the best representation. Here, we use the existing ElasticSearch [16] index dictionary to establish the "element-label" indices. In this way, the label corresponding to an element can be quickly accessed, and we can compare the label with the entity/relation words, and obtain the similarity between them by calculating the cosine similarity.

3.4 Entity/Relation Disambiguation

Connection Density Scoring. The calculation of candidate scores in EEARL is based on the concept of connection density, as proposed by EARL [3]. For a given entity and relation, joint disambiguation is aimed at observing whether the entities and relations in a natural language question are in close proximity in a KB. If two elements are closer, then it is considered that the co-occurrence probability of them in this question is greater. We model the distance in the KB as the connection density, which is defined in terms of the number of connections, the number of hops, and the initial ranking of items based on text similarity. The connection density about the previous example is shown in Fig. 2.

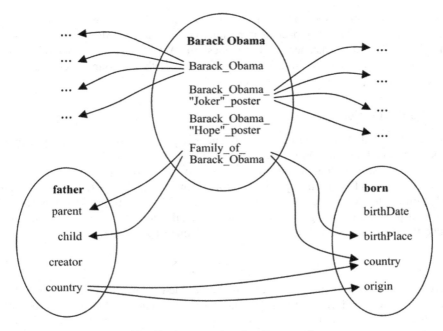

Fig. 2. A connection density example

The number of connections, the number of hops, and the initial ranking of items are further described as follows:

- Assume that for each entity/relation, we generate a candidate element list. Following the relevant practice in EARL [3], the hop distance is defined as the shortest distance (i.e., the number of hops) between two elements in the subdivision graph [3]. Furthermore, it is assumed that there is a lack of semantic connections between two nodes in a KB that are too far apart, so any two nodes with hop count greater than 2 are considered to be disconnected. Thus, the number of connections of a candidate element is defined as the number of connections from it to all candidates in other lists, divided by the number of keyword phrases.
- The hop count of a candidate element is defined as the sum of the distances from the element to all the candidates in the other list, divided by the number of the keyword phrases.
- The initial ranking of an element refers to the ranking of the element in the candidate list when Elastic Search [16] retrieves it.

Once the above three numbers are obtained, we use machine learning to train a classification model for calculating the probability that a candidate becomes the best candidate given a candidate element list. To better tackle the over-fitting problem and shorten model training time, we use xgboost [18] as the classifier. When a candidate element is given, its three numbers are input into the model, and a value between 0 and 1 is obtained as the connection density score, denoted by $score_{connect\_density}$.

Context Scoring. So far, EEARL only considers the connections between all entities and relations in natural language questions, without using other non-entity/non-relation information, which may make the relation linking ambiguity problem difficult to solve effectively. For general natural language questions, the sentences usually contain wh-words like "Where", "When" and "Who", and these wh-words are effective information for solving the ambiguity of the relation. For example, "Where" can restrict the attributes of certain relations to "place", and "When" can limit to "time". Therefore, such information in the context can be leveraged to help improve the accuracy of relation linking.

Because the word-level model preserves the semantics of words in sentences well, EEARL employs a word-level LSTM [5] to convert each non-entity/non-relation vocabulary in the context into a context vector. The training data consist of sequences of words and label vectors. Specifically, we regard all the non-entity/non-relation vocabularies in the question as context, and then use GloVe [19] to convert these words into vectors. Furthermore, a word-level LSTM is used to compress many such vectors into one vector, that is, the context vector. The model for generating the context vector is shown in Fig. 3.

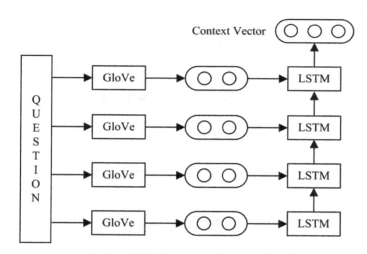

Fig. 3. Context vector generation model

As for feature vectors, we use the embedding models and the LSTM network to convert the domain, range, type, and the local name of relation URI into four vectors respectively. Specifically, we use the GloVe embedding model to transfer the domain, range, and type into three vectors. For the local name of the relation URI, we first split it into segments, and then use GloVe to generate word vectors, and finally adopt a LSTM to compress the word vectors into the fourth vector. Finally, we combine the four vectors to form the feature vector. The feature vector generation model is shown in Fig. 4.

Particularly, for a relation element without domain and/or range, we mine the attributes of the semantically similar words with the relation name to complement the missing part of the feature vector representing the relation. Specifically, we use the character embedding based LSTM [20] to implement missing attributes, because this model can handle the OOV words more effectively. The network used to complete the domain/range vectors is illustrated in Fig. 5.

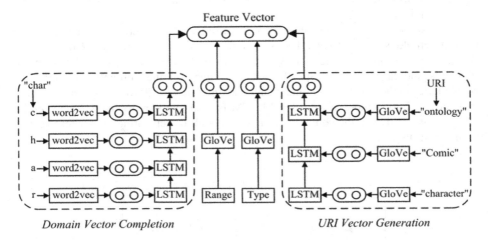

Feature Vector

Domain Vector Completion   *URI Vector Generation*

Fig. 4. Feature vector generation model

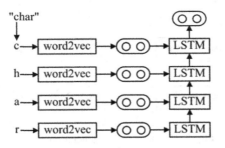

Fig. 5. Domain/range vector completion model

Given a natural language question, we use the LSTM network to predict the context vector (Fig. 3), and adopt the feature vector generation model (Fig. 4) to represent the feature vector for each candidate element. After that, we calculate the similarity between the context vector and the feature vector as the context score, denoted by $score_{context}$. This indicates that, in addition to the original connection density-based score, we also consider the impact of context information on relation linking. The final score of a candidate element is a weighted aggregation of the two scores, as defined by Eq. (2):

$$score' = (1 - \beta) \times score_{connect\_density} + \beta \times score_{context} \qquad (2)$$

where β is empirically set to 0.4.

3.5 Adaptive Learning

The aforementioned methods split the entire process into multiple separate modules, and there is no feedback between these modules to correct the results. In other words, if the previous module produces an error, the error would gradually increase as the process progresses, with a larger impact on the final results.

In order to enable mutual feedback between the modules, we use the adaptive learning method [3] in EARL to correct errors. In the linking process, when the score based on connection density is less than a predefined threshold, the entity/relation type of the keyword phrase should be changed, and the modules after the entity/relation prediction are then re-executed. As in EARL, the threshold is set to 0.01. The schematic diagram of the adaptive learning is illustrated in Fig. 6.

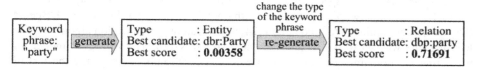

Fig. 6. Schematic diagram of the adaptive learning

4 Experiments and Discussion

4.1 Experimental Design

Experimental Datasets. We conducted the experiments using two typical benchmark datasets: LC-QuAD [6] and QALD-7 [7]. We briefly introduce them below:

- LC-QuAD is the Large-Scale Complex Question Answering Dataset widely used for assessing the robustness and accuracy of KBQA systems. It is a dataset with 5,000 questions and their corresponding SPARQL queries over the DBpedia dataset (2016-04 release) [6].
- QALD-7, the 7th instantiation of Question Answering over Linked Data (QALD) at ESWC 2017, is a standard evaluation benchmark for assessing and comparing QALD systems. The data in QALD-7 is also based on the DBpedia dataset (2016-04 release) [7].

Evaluation Tasks and Metric. We evaluated and compared EEARL with EARL [3] and several baseline methods on entity linking and relation linking. For entity linking, the chosen baseline methods include AGDISTIS [10], Spotlight [21], and Babelfy [22].

AGDISTIS is based on graph disambiguation. Spotlight uses the surface forms of entities for disambiguation, while Babelfy uses the word senses of entities for linking them to a KB. For relation linking, the selected baseline methods are ReMatch [11] and RelMatch [12]. For both entity linking and relation linking, we used accuracy as the evaluation metric, which refers to the proportion of correctly-identified entities/relations in the total number of entities/relations.

Implementation and Parameter Settings. For EARL, we directly reused its Python code published in [3] (cf. https://github.com/AskNowQA/EARL). We implemented EEARL by modifying the entity/relation disambiguation part of EARL's code. The experimental setup and source code of EEARL are publicly available in Github (cf. https://github.com/Vodkazy/EEARL). For the baseline methods, we took the results from [3], as both experiments used the same experimental setup including datasets.

The following describes the parameter settings for EEARL. The hidden layer size of the character-level LSTM network for entity/relation prediction was 128, and the sizes of the two fully-connected layers were 256 and 512, respectively. The LSTM network used the vectors trained by RDF2Vec [23] as the pre-training data, and executed Adam [24] as the training optimization algorithm. The learning rate was set to 0.0001, and the batch size was 128.

The LSTM network for domain completion and range completion had hidden layers of 269 and 206, respectively, and the fully-connected layer was a layer with size of 50. The LSTM network used the data with domain or range attributes from DBpedia [25] for model training. We used Adam [24] as the training optimization algorithm. The learning rate was set to 0.001, and the batch size was 128. The word2vec model for predicting the domains used pre-trained character-level embedding, while the rest of GloVe used word-level embedding.

The LSTM network used to calculate the context vector was trained using the QALD-6 dataset [26]. The hidden layer size of the LSTM network was 128, and the two fully-connected layers were 256 and 200, respectively. The training optimization algorithm was Adam [24]. The learning rate was 0.001, and the batch size was 128.

4.2   Experimental Results

The accuracy results of entity linking are shown in Table 1. Observing the results, we can find that EEARL is slightly better than EARL and outperforms the three baseline methods in terms of entity linking accuracy.

Table 1. Accuracy results of entity linking.

Methods	LC-QuAD	QALD-7
FOX [27] + AGDISTIS [10]	0.36	0.30
DBpedia Spotlight [21]	0.40	0.42
Babelfy [22]	0.56	0.56
EARL [3] without adaptive learning	0.61	0.55
EARL with adaptive learning	0.65	0.57
EEARL without adaptive learning	0.62	0.55
EEARL with adaptive learning	**0.65**	**0.58**

The accuracy results of relation linking are shown in Table 2. Observing the results, we can find that EEARL is better than EARL (accuracy increased by 3%) and far better than the two baseline methods in terms of relation linking accuracy.

Table 2. Accuracy results of relation linking.

Method	LC-QuAD	QALD-7
ReMatch [11]	0.12	0.31
RelMatch [12]	0.15	0.29
EARL [3] without adaptive learning	0.32	0.45
EARL with adaptive learning	0.36	0.47
EEARL without adaptive learning	0.34	0.47
EEARL with adaptive learning	**0.38**	**0.50**

Additionally, Table 2 indicates that the accuracy results of relation linking on LC-QuAD and QALD-7 are quite different. This is due to the fact that the questions in LC-QuAD are more complex than those in QALD-7. Besides, Tables 1 and 2 confirm that adaptive learning can significantly help improve the performance.

4.3 Discussion

According to the results, the improvement of EEARL was mainly reflected in the treatment of wh-words. For example, given a question "Where were Justina Machado and John Englehard born?" in LC-QuAD, EARL actually ignored "Where" and thus incorrectly linked "born" to dbp:birthDate. Differently, EEARL considered the effect of "Where" on "born" and correctly linked "born" to dbp:birthPlace.

On the other hand, our method still has a few limitations. For instance, when handling relation linking, it is difficult to distinguish between elements of class type and property type, resulting in errors in relation mapping. Furthermore, our method cannot deal with inference and restrictions. For questions such as "Who is the tallest man in China?", EEARL fails to deal with the "tallest" restriction and only links "man" to dbr:Person. However, this problem can be deferred until the subsequent query generation phase [28], which can be simplified in the linking phase.

5 Conclusion

In this paper, we have proposed an improved joint entity and relation linking method called EEARL, which leverages full context information to improve linking accuracy. When generating relation linking, EEARL considers not only the impact of entities and relations co-occurred in the natural language questions, but also the impact of other non-entity/non-relation vocabularies in the questions. Our experimental results on two benchmark datasets show that EEARL outperforms EARL and several baseline methods in terms of entity linking and relation linking accuracy. In future work, we look forward to improving the accuracy of entity/relation prediction and exploring external information outside KBs.

References

1. Berant, J., Chou, A., Frostig, R., Liang, P.: Semantic parsing on Freebase from question-answer pairs. In: Proceedings of the 2013 Conference on Empirical Methods in Natural Language Processing, EMNLP 2013, pp. 1533–1544. Association for Computational Linguistics (2013). https://www.aclweb.org/anthology/D13-1160

2. Kolitsas, N., Ganea, O.-E., Hofmann, T.: End-to-end neural entity linking. In: Proceedings of the 22nd Conference on Computational Natural Language Learning, CoNLL 2018, pp. 519–529. Association for Computational Linguistics (2018). https://aclweb.org/anthology/papers/K/K18/K18-1050/

3. Dubey, M., Banerjee, D., Chaudhuri, D., Lehmann, J.: EARL: joint entity and relation linking for question answering over knowledge graphs. In: Vrandečić, D., et al. (eds.) ISWC 2018. LNCS, vol. 11136, pp. 108–126. Springer, Cham (2018). https://doi.org/10.1007/978-3-030-00671-6_7

4. Pintea, C.-M., Pop, P.C., Chira, C.: The generalized traveling salesman problem solved with ant algorithms. Complex Adapt. Syst. Model. **5**, 8 (2017). https://doi.org/10.1186/s40294-017-0048-9

5. Lukovnikov, D., Fischer, A., Lehmann, J., Auer, S.: Neural network-based question answering over knowledge graphs on word and character level. In: Proceedings of the 26th International Conference on World Wide Web, WWW 2017, pp. 1211–1220. International World Wide Web Conferences Steering Committee (2017). https://doi.org/10.1145/3038912.3052675

6. Trivedi, P., Maheshwari, G., Dubey, M., Lehmann, J.: LC-QuAD: a corpus for complex question answering over knowledge graphs. In: d'Amato, C., et al. (eds.) ISWC 2017. LNCS, vol. 10588, pp. 210–218. Springer, Cham (2017). https://doi.org/10.1007/978-3-319-68204-4_22

7. Usbeck, R., Ngomo, A.-C.N., Haarmann, B., Krithara, A., Röder, M., Napolitano, G.: 7th open challenge on question answering over linked data (QALD-7). In: Dragoni, M., Solanki, M., Blomqvist, E. (eds.) SemWebEval 2017. CCIS, vol. 769, pp. 59–69. Springer, Cham (2017). https://doi.org/10.1007/978-3-319-69146-6_6

8. Ratinov, L., Roth, D., Downey, D., Anderson, M.: Local and global algorithms for disambiguation to Wikipedia. In: The 49th Annual Meeting of the Association for Computational Linguistics: Human Language Technologies, Proceedings of the Conference, pp. 1375–1384. Association for Computational Linguistics (2011). https://www.aclweb.org/anthology/P11-1138

9. Yang, Y., Chang, M.-W.: S-MART: novel tree-based structured learning algorithms applied to tweet entity linking. In: Proceedings of the 53rd Annual Meeting of the Association for Computational Linguistics, ACL 2015, vol. 1, pp. 504–513. The Association for Computer Linguistics (2015). https://www.aclweb.org/anthology/P15-1049

10. Usbeck, R., et al.: AGDISTIS - graph-based disambiguation of named entities using linked data. In: Mika, P., et al. (eds.) ISWC 2014. LNCS, vol. 8796, pp. 457–471. Springer, Cham (2014). https://doi.org/10.1007/978-3-319-11964-9_29

11. Mulang, I.O., Singh, K., Orlandi, F.: Matching natural language relations to knowledge graph properties for question answering. In: Proceedings of the 13th International Conference on Semantic Systems, SEMANTICS 2017, pp. 89–96. ACM (2017). https://doi.org/10.1145/3132218.3132229

12. Singh, K., et al.: Capturing knowledge in semantically-typed relational patterns to enhance relation linking. In: Proceedings of the Knowledge Capture Conference, K-CAP 2017, Article No. 31, pp. 31:1–31:8. ACM (2017). https://doi.org/10.1145/3148011.3148031

13. Miller, G.A., Fellbaum, C.: WordNet then and now. Lang. Res. Eval. **41**(2), 209–214 (2007). https://doi.org/10.1007/s10579-007-9044-6
14. Xu, K., Zhang, S., Feng, Y., Zhao, D.: Answering natural language questions via phrasal semantic parsing. In: Zong, C., Nie, J.Y., Zhao, D., Feng, Y. (eds.) Natural Language Processing and Chinese Computing. CCIS, vol. 496, pp. 333–344. Springer, Heidelberg (2014). https://doi.org/10.1007/978-3-662-45924-9_30
15. Collobert, R., Weston, J., Bottou, L., Karlen, M., Kavukcuoglu, K., Kuksa, P.P.: Natural language processing (almost) from scratch. J. Mach. Learn. Res. **12**, 2493–2537 (2011). https://dl.acm.org/citation.cfm?id=2078186
16. Akdal, B., ÇabukKeskin, Z.G., Ekinci, E.E., Kardas, G.: Model-driven query generation for ElasticSearch. In: Proceedings of the 2018 Federated Conference on Computer Science and Information Systems, FedCSIS 2018, pp. 853–862. IEEE (2018). https://doi.org/10.15439/2018F218
17. Pinter, Y., Guthrie, R., Eisenstein, J.: Mimicking word embeddings using subword RNNs. In: Proceedings of the 2017 Conference on Empirical Methods in Natural Language Processing, EMNLP 2017, pp. 102–112. Association for Computational Linguistics (2017). https://www.aclweb.org/anthology/D17-1010
18. Chen, T., Guestrin, C.: XGBoost: a scalable tree boosting system. In: Proceedings of the 22nd ACM SIGKDD International Conference on Knowledge Discovery and Data Mining, KDD 2016, pp. 785–794. Association for Computing Machinery (2017). https://doi.org/10.1145/2939672.2939785
19. Pennington, J., Socher, R., Manning, C.D.: GloVe: global vectors for word representation. In: Proceedings of the 2014 Conference on Empirical Methods in Natural Language Processing, EMNLP 2014, pp. 1532–1543. Association for Computational Linguistics (2014). https://www.aclweb.org/anthology/D14-1162
20. Zou, L., Huang, R., Wang, H., Yu, J.X., He, W., Zhao, D.: Natural language question answering over RDF - a graph data driven approach. In: Proceedings of the ACM SIGMOD International Conference on Management of Data, SIGMOD 2014, pp. 313–324. ACM (2014). https://doi.org/10.1145/2588555.2610525
21. Mendes, P.N., Jakob, M., García-Silva, A., Bizer, C.: DBpedia spotlight: shedding light on the web of documents. In: Proceedings the 7th International Conference on Semantic Systems, I-SEMANTICS 2011, pp. 1–8. ACM (2011). https://doi.org/10.1145/2063518.2063519
22. Moro, A., Raganato, A., Navigli, R.: Entity linking meets word sense disambiguation: a unified approach. Trans. Assoc. Comput. Linguist. **2**, 231–244 (2014). https://transacl.org/ojs/index.php/tacl/article/view/291
23. Ristoski, P., Paulheim, H.: RDF2Vec: RDF graph embeddings for data mining. In: Groth, P., et al. (eds.) ISWC 2016. LNCS, vol. 9981, pp. 498–514. Springer, Cham (2016). https://doi.org/10.1007/978-3-319-46523-4_30
24. Kingma, D.P., Ba, J.: Adam: a method for stochastic optimization. In: 3rd International Conference on Learning Representations, ICLR 2015, Conference Track Proceedings. https://arxiv.org/abs/1412.6980
25. Boiński, T., Szymański, J., Dudek, B., Zalewski, P., Dompke, S., Czarnecka, M.: DBpedia and YAGO based system for answering questions in natural language. In: Nguyen, N.T., Pimenidis, E., Khan, Z., Trawiński, B. (eds.) ICCCI 2018. LNCS (LNAI), vol. 11055, pp. 383–392. Springer, Cham (2018). https://doi.org/10.1007/978-3-319-98443-8_35

26. Unger, C., Ngomo, A.-C.N., Cabrio, E.: 6th open challenge on question answering over linked data (QALD-6). In: Sack, H., Dietze, S., Tordai, A., Lange, C. (eds.) SemWebEval 2016. CCIS, vol. 641, pp. 171–177. Springer, Cham (2016). https://doi.org/10.1007/978-3-319-46565-4_13

27. Speck, R., Ngomo, A.-C. N.: Ensemble learning of named entity recognition algorithms using multilayer perceptron for the multilingual web of data. In: Proceedings of the Knowledge Capture Conference, K-CAP 2017, Article No. 26, pp. 26:1–26:4. ACM (2017). https://doi.org/10.1145/3148011.3154471

28. Zafar, H., Napolitano, G., Lehmann, J.: Formal query generation for question answering over knowledge bases. In: Gangemi, A., et al. (eds.) ESWC 2018. LNCS, vol. 10843, pp. 714–728. Springer, Cham (2018). https://doi.org/10.1007/978-3-319-93417-4_46

Community Detection in Knowledge Graph Network with Matrix Factorization Learning

Xiaohua Shi[1,2](✉)(ID), Yin Qian[1](ID), and Hongtao Lu[2](ID)

[1] Library, Shanghai Jiaotong University, Shanghai, China
xhshi@sjtu.edu.cn
[2] Department of Computer Science, Shanghai JiaoTong University,
Shanghai, China

Abstract. Recently, knowledge graph is one of most hot topics in artificial intelligence research area, we may find that data in knowledge graph analysis shows vast network structure features. In this paper, we investigate some main methods of current network analysis and community detection tasks related with knowledge graph and semantic network. Comparing with relevant network community detection methods in various semantic network data, our matrix factorization learning method achieves good performance for community detection.

Keywords: Knowledge graph · Semantic network · Network analysis · Community detection · Matrix factorization learning

1 Introduction

Since May 2012, Google released the project of Knowledge Graph (KG), and announced that they would build next generation of intelligent search engine based on KG. Main purpose of Knowledge Graph was to transform search from string to data association application, and improve relevance of knowledge query results and overall search experience by using graphical connection and contextual data. The success of Knowledge Graph and its application to semantic technology has led to the reuse of this term to describe similar projects in semantic research. Key technologies of Knowledge Graph include extracting entities and their attribute information from web pages of the Internet, as well as relationships graph or network between named entities [28].

Knowledge Graphs capture facts related to people, processes, applications, data and things, and the relationships among them. They also capture evidence that can be used to attribute the strengths of these relationships, where the context is derived from. With the extensive development and application of artificial intelligence technology in scientific research and practice, Knowledge Graphs have been developing rapidly as an important subject of artificial intelligence, promoting in-depth with machine learning applications and innovation

J. Song and X. Zhu (Eds.): APWeb-WAIM 2019 Workshops, LNCS 11809, pp. 37–51, 2019.
https://doi.org/10.1007/978-3-030-33982-1_4

of knowledge [16]. Knowledge Graphs connect all kinds of information together to form a relational network, and provide the ability to analyze problems from a relational perspective. Therefore, Knowledge Graphs can also be understood as structured semantic knowledge base networks that allow people and machines to make better use of the connections in their data.

The main applications of knowledge graph will include knowledge fusion, semantic network, semantic search and recommendation, Q&A and dialogue system, and big data analysis and decision-making [1]. In the field of computer science and artificial intelligence, "knowledge graphs are essentially the knowledge base of Semantic Network", and in the field of knowledge engineering and application, knowledge graphs can be understood as multi-relational graph network.

Community Detection, as one of methods in network analysis [2], is mainly as a research method and research perspective application of various disciplines, such as social networks, trading networks, biological networks, collaborative network and semantic network, etc. In network community detection applications, relation of each nodes in graph-based network are nonnegative due to their physical nature. The adjacency matrix $\mathbf{A}$ as well as the Laplacian matrix completely represents the structure of network. Using Matrix Factorization learning methods to obtain new representations of network can achieve much productive effect in network community analysis [18,42]. It is likely an efficient network partition tool to find the communities because of its powerful interpretability and close relationship with other clustering methods. Community detection with Matrix Factorization learning can capture the underlying structure of network in the low dimensional data space with its community-based representation, and achieve good performance in many different type networks.

In this paper, we will introduce and analyze the main techniques and methods of network analysis in the aspects of semantic network, and apply Matrix Factorization Learning methods in community detection tasks in related knowledge graph network datasets.

2   Related Works

Graphical structure of knowledge can be regarded as a knowledge of different sources to build the model of system integration [33]. Knowledge graph has many similar characteristics of semantic network, and their main difference is that knowledge graph data source is extensive, focus more attention to knowledge representation and knowledge fusion technology. Knowledge graphs allow users to quickly view relevant information without further searching. The main benefit of the graph is that the connection relations between nodes are mutual in the data format, users can easily access new data items, and the relationship between groups of inactive regions can be easily discovered by traversing the links from a network.

Paulheim [26] introduces some of the most popular knowledge graphs on the Semantic Web, and discuss how machine learning is used to improve those knowledge graphs, and how they can be exploited as background knowledge in popular machine learning tasks, such as recommender systems. Ji *et al.* [15] propose a more fine-grained model, they use two vectors to represent a named symbol object (entity and relation). The first one represents the meaning of an entity relation, the other one is used to construct mapping matrix dynamically. Henk *et al.* [14] formulate the task of scholarly recommendation as a link prediction task based on knowledge graph embeddings. A knowledge graph containing scholarly metadata is created and enriched with textual descriptions.

As shown in Fig. 1, according to the Max Planck institute in Germany explained, network analysis has been deeply integrated into quantitative analysis of social knowledge research area. Meanwhile, semantic model used to describe data and its structure has also become an increasingly popular way of heterogeneous data combination and analysis. The corresponding structure is knowledge graph network. Both methods describe and analyze networked data, with the former focusing on dynamic change and its driving force, and the latter on the semantic feature of various networks.

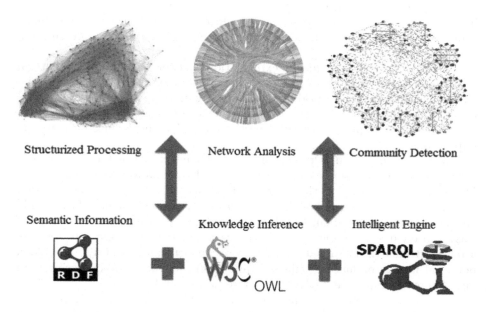

Fig. 1. Knowledge graph model and network analysis methods.

In the process of generating knowledge graphs, there will be problems such as the reliability of generating relations, the frequency of different entities appearing at the same time, and the change of entity attributes, which can be handled by network science. Knowledge graph is a method of storage and use of data, which mainly contains nodes and edges as network data structure. KGs describe the physical world in the form of symbol of concepts and their mutual relations, its basic composition unit is 'entity - relationship - entities' triples, as well as the entity and its related to 'attribute - value' relations, through the relationship between different entities connected, we can constitute the knowledge structure graph or network. In a knowledge graph network, each node represents the 'entity' of the real world, and each edge represents the relationship between entities.

In artificial intelligence related solutions, we may combine method of network science and knowledge graph model for further research. Adding knowledge model in network science will be more help to understand the network structure of semantic features and potential tacit knowledge. Also in knowledge graph research, we can introduce network scientific analysis, such as community detection, to obtain more quantitative data in the interaction and reasoning of knowledge, enhancing knowledge graph topological simplification, reduce overall computation efficiency, and promote the perspective effect for visual display.

Yang et al. [41] propose that network representation learning aims at learning distributed vector representation for each vertex in a network, which is also increasingly recognized as an important aspect for network analysis. Most network representation learning methods investigate network structures for learning. In reality, network vertices contain rich information (such as text), which cannot be well applied with algorithmic frameworks of typical representation learning methods.

According to bales et al. [3] explaination, network generated by natural language has the topological properties common to other natural phenomena. Therefore, through small-world features and scale-free topologies, as well as various network analysis methods, the development of control vocabulary in large-scale knowledge graphs and feature description in given fields have been greatly improved.

Matrix Factorization (Decomposition) Learning is one of the most widely used method in Machine Learning, its main goal is to transfer the original data Matrix to be expressed as the product of two or more low rank Matrix form, after the decomposition of Matrix rank is far less than the original Matrix rank, and application of low rank low dimension Matrix that deal with all kinds of classification and clustering task. In recent years, more and more researchers pay attention to matrix factorization applications, which can efficiently find hidden potential factors or missing values in prediction matrix by decomposing data into different compact and effective representation methods.

In community detection applications, relation of each nodes in graph-based network are nonnegative due to their physical nature. The adjacency matrix $\mathbf{A}$ as well as the Laplacian matrix completely represents the structure of network, and $\mathbf{A}$ is non-negative naturally. Based on the consideration that there is no any physical meaning to reconstruct a network with negative adjacency matrix, using Nonnegative Matrix Factorization (NMF) to obtain new representations of network with non-negativity constraints can achieve much productive effect in community analysis [18,42].

Semantic networks are a typical type of network data representation incorporating linguistic information that describes concepts or objects and the relationship or dependency between them. Network community structure, or module organization, is an important attribute of real world network, which is generally considered as an important factor to study the system functional characteristics of network. Network Community Detection methods [19] are to use the node information, the relationships between different communities were found in a static network. The underlying assumption is that the interaction within the community is much closer than that between communities. In other words, the points in the same community have a certain strong correlation, while the points between different communities have a corresponding weak correlation. Community discovery is a very meaningful thing. To implement community discovery operation on a large network is to divide it according to some standards. On this basis, each community can be further explored. From the perspective of computing, community partitioning of knowledge network is equivalent to decomposing the task of the whole global network, and plays a role in reducing computational complexity.

Jose et al. [23] developed a method to apply community detection algorithm to semantic Web data graph analysis, identifying different community groups from DBpedia database data network. Han *et al.*[13] proposed a clustering community detection algorithm based on the pso-lda model for the community discovery problem of semantic social networks.

Wu [27] put forward a community detection method based on the path of semantic heterogeneous, through semantic paths to measure different types of heterogeneous information similarity between objects, and then to construct reliability matrix, as a semi-supervised regularization constraint of the nonnegative matrix decomposition, thus achieve heterogeneous network community, the proposed method can more accurately found in the heterogeneous network community structure. Kianian [17] proposed a new semantic community detection method that focuses on user attributes rather than network topology.

Bhatt [4] proposed a community detection and feature description algorithm for fusing knowledge graphs. The algorithm fuses the context information of node attributes described by multiple knowledge domain specific hierarchical concept maps, finds the context that can best summarize the nodes in the community, and finds the community that is consistent with the context of the generalized community.

At present, many scholars have conducted community detection application and research on semantic web. Xia *et al.* [38] constructed semantic networks using semantic information extracted from comments and focused on the 'giant components' of online social networks to reduce computational complexity. The real data sets are compared with the annotation-based interactive method. Xin *et al.* [44] proposed a random walk based overlapping community discovery algorithm for semantic social network. This algorithm builds semantic space based on LDA algorithm, and takes semantic impact model and weighted adjacency matrix as parameters to propose an improved random walk algorithm for overlapping community discovery of semantic social network. Ereteo *et al.* [11] proposed a community detection algorithm SemTagP using semantic data captured when constructing RDF graphs of social networks. The algorithm not only realizes the community discovery function, but also marks the community by using the markers that people use in the process of social markers and the semantic relations inferred between the markers.

3 Application of Semantic Network Quantitative Analysis

The semantic network is often used as a form of knowledge representation, which is actually a directed graph. Vertices represent concepts, while edges represent semantic relationships between concepts. Take scientific semantic network structure composed of research links and keywords as an example:

Article A is connected with article B, where the name of article A is the entry point of article B.

Data structure in the knowledge graph is a real graph or network, and in the proper mathematical sense allows for further application of various network science analysis methods (such as shortest path computing or network analysis methods), which add an additional network analysis perspective to the stored data.

The network analysis method [9] is mainly based on the network model which uses points to represent the elements of the network and edges to represent the relationship and interaction between nodes, and studies the quantitative properties, topological structure and evolution process of the network. Classic models such as 'principles of a small world' [36] and 'scale-free characteristic' [25] have been widely used in semantic network analysis of various knowledge graphs.

By calculating attribute of knowledge graph network, the computational efficiency of knowledge graph method can be effectively improved by applying network clustering algorithm, we can identify the relationship between unconnected components or concepts as an indicator of missing relationship. We can also calculate the diameter of knowledge graph network as a general or specific indicator of knowledge graph network.

Steyvers et al. [32] respectively conduct quantitative network analysis on word association network, WordNet and Roget thesaurus network, and prove that they all have small-world structure and follow power law distribution. Li Mei et al. [21] analyzed the semantic search of peer-to-peer (P2P) resources with a large amount of data, and designed the semantic small-world method, so as to realize efficient semantic search in P2P system. The method is mainly based on three design ideas: small world network, semantic clustering and data dimension reduction.

$$P(z) \sim z^{-\tau} \tag{1}$$

Bernat et al. [8] and Graham et al. [35] respectively carried out quantitative network analysis on semantic Web ontology data, semantic database data of language education and Wikipedia page data.

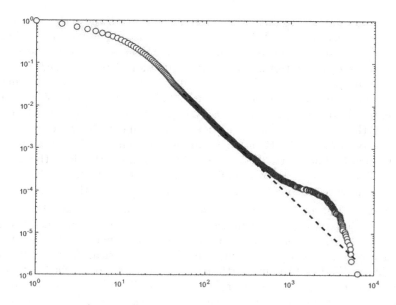

Fig. 2. Node degree fitting curve of Google Web semantic network.

We select KG example data from Google, which was a part of the Google programming contest Web data released in 2002[1], to quantitative analysis of the relevant network experiment, where nodes represent web pages and directional edges represent hyperlinks between them. The total number of nodes in these data is 875,713, and the number of edges is 5,105,039. The average clustering coefficient calculated is 0.5143, and the maximum diameter length is 21. We use MATLAB PLFIT toolbox[2] Law fitting to Pow, access to the Formula 1. And related fitting chart in Fig. 2 has been marked by a dotted line Power Law distribution and distribution parameters is 2.9, thus we can check that general knowledge graph data networks are scale-free feature.

4   Our Matrix Factorization Method

Given a set of points $\mathbf{x}_1, \mathbf{x}_2, \cdots, \mathbf{x}_n$, they form the matrix $\mathbf{X} = [\mathbf{x}_1, \mathbf{x}_2, \cdots, \mathbf{x}_n] \in \mathbf{R}^{m \times n}$, where $\mathbf{x}_j$, $j = 1, \cdots, n$, is an m-dimensional non-negative vector, denoting the j-th data point. NMF aims to factorize $\mathbf{X}$ into the product of two non-negative matrices $\mathbf{U}$ and $\mathbf{V}$. The product of $\mathbf{U}$ and $\mathbf{V}^T$ is expected to be a good approximation to the original matrix, *i.e.*,

$$\mathbf{X} \approx \mathbf{U}\mathbf{V}^T \tag{2}$$

---

[1] https://snap.stanford.edu/data/web-Google.html.
[2] http://www.santafe.edu/~aaronc/powerlaws.

The size of the factorized matrices $\mathbf{U}$ and $\mathbf{V}$ are $m \times k$ and $n \times k$, respectively. The dimensionality of $\mathbf{U}$ and $\mathbf{V}$ is k. In most NMF algorithms, the dimensionality k of the factorized matrices is given, and we should set k to be the same as known count of communities in community detection situation. Each column of decomposed matrix $\mathbf{U}$ can be regarded as the center of one network community, and each node can be represented by an additive combination of all column vectors of the decomposed matrix $\mathbf{U}$. Each entry in the j-th row of the factorized matrix $\mathbf{V}$ is the projection of the j-th node $\mathbf{x}_j$ of the matrix $\mathbf{X}$ onto corresponding column vector of matrix $\mathbf{U}$. Hence, the community membership of each node can be determined by finding the basis (one column of $\mathbf{U}$) with which the node has the largest projection value. We examine each row of learning (coefficient) matrix $\mathbf{V}$, and assign node $\mathbf{x}_j$ to community c if $c = \arg\max_c v_{jc}$ [31].

In order to obtain two non-negative matrices, we can quantify the quality of the approximation by using a cost function with some distance metric to compare the observation and the prior component. Generally we use β-Divergence $\mathbf{D}_\beta(\mathbf{X}; \mathbf{UV^T})$ [12] in a bayesian statistical framework. When $\beta = 0, 1, 2$, $\mathbf{D}_\beta(\mathbf{X}; \mathbf{UV^T})$ is proportional to the (negative) log-likelihood of the Itakara-Saito (IS), Kullback-Leibler (KL) and Euclidean noise models up to a constant. We assume that there exists a noise E with bayesian inference between $\mathbf{X}$ and $\mathbf{UV^T}$.

$$\mathbf{X} = \mathbf{UV^T} + \mathbf{E} \tag{3}$$

Schmidt *et al.* [30] present a Bayesian treatment of NMF based on a normal likelihood and exponential priors, and approximate the posterior density of the NMF factors. This model equals to minimize the squares Euclidean distance $\mathbf{D_2}(\mathbf{X}; \mathbf{UV^T})$ for NMF. We assume the noise $\mathbf{E}$ is i.i.d Gaussian with variance σ_n^2, and the likelihood can be written as:

$$P(X|U,V) = \left(\frac{-1}{\sqrt{2\pi}\sigma_r}\right)^{MN} \prod_i \prod_j \frac{1}{\sqrt{2\pi}\sigma_r} e^{\left\{\frac{1}{2}\left(\frac{X_{ij} - [UV^T]_{ij}}{\sigma_r}\right)^2\right\}} \tag{4}$$

As shown in Algorithmn 1, we cooperate a statistical *shrinkage* method in a Bayesian framework to find the number of communities and build a model selection based on Automatic Relevance Determination (ARD). We propose a Bayesian Symmetric NMF (BSNMF) method [39], and principally iterate out s_{ik} with gradual change in update rule of S. The prior will try to promote a *shrinkage* to zero of s_{ik} with a rate constant proportional to β_k in update rule of β_k. A large β_k represents a belief that the half-normal distribution over s_{ik} has small variance, and hence s_{ik} is expected to get close to zero. We can see the priors and the likelihood function (quantifying how well we explain real data) are combined with the effect that columns of S which have little effect in changing how well we explain the observed data will shrink close to zero. We can effectively estimate the communities number K_C by computer the non-zero column number from S.

Algorithm 1. BSNMF Process

Require: Network Adjacent Matrix $X \in \mathbb{R}_+^{n \times n}$, Initialized factorization Dimension K, and Fixed Hyperparameter a,b

Ensure: $K_c S_c$

1: Define a Diagonal Matrix $B \in \mathbb{R}_+^{K \times K}$ with diagonal line as β_k
2: **for** $i = 1 \to n_{iter}$ **do**
3:      $S \leftarrow \left(\frac{S}{1*S+S*B} \right) \left[\left(\frac{X}{S*S^T} \right) * S^T \right]$
4:      $\beta_k \leftarrow \frac{N+a_k-1}{\frac{1}{2}\sum_i s_{ij}^2 + b_k}$
5: **end for**
6: $K_c \leftarrow$ Nonzero columns number in S
7: $S_c \leftarrow$ Delete zero columns from S

---

5   Experiment Results

5.1   Expriments in DBLP Network

Semantic concept-based and knowledge graph analysis can be combined with topological analysis of online communities to better understand the community structure in complex networks. Performing community detection on knowledge ontologies to understand its network structure. If there are communities within the network, where the nodes are not connected to the rest that would indicate that the ontology lacks cohesion. We can use weakly connected components to help identify if the ontology contains any unrelated community of concepts.

In this section, we use DBLP (DataBase systems and Logic Programming) ground-truth scientific co-author dataset[3] to evaluate non-overlapping community detection result with different methods. The DBLP computer science bibliography dataset contains large number of authors to provide a comprehensive list of research papers in computer science. In DBLP co-authorship network, two authors are connected if they publish at least one paper together. We define publication venue, e.g., journal or conference, as an individual ground-truth community from practical significance [43]. Authors who published to a certain journal or conference will form one community. We regard each connected component in a group as a separate ground-truth community. We select a large DBLP network with 4,946 ground-truth communities, and it contains 42,591 nodes and 133,092 links.

We compare our algorithm with other seven state-of-the-art community detection methods, and all eight algorithms are listed below. Algorithm 5 to 8 are Matrix Factorization Learning methods, and Algorithm 2, 5, 6 should be given communities dimension first. Some of them have been applied in community detection tasks before.

1. Greedy community detection (GCD) agglomerative method which takes into account the heterogeneity of community size observed in real networks [10].

---

[3] http://snap.stanford.edu/data/com-DBLP.html.

2. Spectral Clustering (SC) make use of the spectrum (eigenvalues) of the similarity matrix of the data to perform dimensionality reduction before clustering in fewer dimensions [22].
3. Louvain (BGLL) can compute high modularity partitions and hierarchies of large networks in quick time [5,24].
4. Greedy modularity optimisation (GMO) algorithm based on the multi-scale algorithm but optimised for modularity [20].
5. Non-negative Matrix Factorization (NMF) based on clustering to be used in community detection [40].
6. Symmetric Non-negative Matrix Factorization (SNMF) for undirected network [37].
7. Bayesian Non-negative Matrix Factorization (BNMF) with Poisson likelihood [7].
8. Bayesian Symmetric Non-negative Matrix Factorization (BSNMF) with Poisson likelihood.

We use three metrics accuracy (AC), normalized mutual information (NMI) and Modularity to evaluate community detection performance on each experiment [6,24,34,40]. Experimental results may been evaluated by comparing the community label of each sample node with its label provided by the ground-truth network.

In matrix factorization learning methods NMF, SNMF, BNMF and BSNMF, we apply 10 independent experiments and every experiment iterates for 500 times. The initial community count k of BNMF and BSNMF is set to $n/10$. In methods SPC, NMF and SNMF K is set to the ground-truth communities number $4,946$, and other 5 methods can spontaneously compute communities count in algorithm itself, such as our method BSNMF with ARD capturing $1,788$ communities.

Table 1 shows the detailed AC, NMI and Q values on the DBLP undirected network. From this result, we can see that BSNMF with symmetric transformation and Bayesian inference promote the three indicators than SNMF and BNMF. Our BSNMF method achieves the best performance, especially in AC and NMI metric. GMO algorithm catch the highest Modularity Q with 0.9217.

5.2   Experiments in Real Chinese Journals Collaborative Network

Through the RSS aggregation source[4] of China journal network, we obtained the papers and author information from four journals subjected in library and intelligence science from 2012 to 2016, including journal of "Information and Documentation Services", "Information studies: Theory & Application", "Information Science" and "Journal of Intelligence". we collect 6,254 papers, which correspond to 14,312 authors. The author's name combined with the author's organization was taken as the de-weighting condition, and the de-weighting was 7625 authors. If every two authors jointly publish a paper, then there is an edge

---

[4] http://rss.cnki.net/rss/.

Table 1. Results of DBLP Communities with Ground-truth

Methods	AC	NMI	Modularity
GCD	0.6334	0.6784	0.7467
SPC	0.5409	0.6156	0.7192
BGLL	0.7429	0.8278	0.8585
GMO	0.7877	0.8616	**0.9217**
NMF	0.5595	0.6253	0.7219
SNMF	0.7377	0.7866	0.8011
BNMF	0.6877	0.7308	0.7815
BSNMF	**0.7904**	**0.8782**	0.9184

Table 2. Results of Real Chinese Journals Co-author network

Methods	Modularity
3-Klique	0.3579
GN	0.5530
BGLL	0.8294
GMO	0.9165
NMF	0.4209
SNMF	0.8165
BSNMF	**0.9664**

between the two points, and the weight of the edge is the number of papers cooperated by the two authors. Accordingly, a large-scale scientific knowledge collaborative network with 7,625 nodes and 12,672 edges is formed, in which the average degree of each node is 1.66, that is, each person and 1.66 person-times of peers in five years carry out cooperative publication.

Due to different researchers published papers, if an author fully publish as an individual author, and their co-author network as an independent node. There are totally 665 isolated nodes in this network, so before community detection application, we can delete these isolated node first, to enhance the result that with no further effect of the whole network. The new cooperative network X is 6960 nodes, and the number of edges is still 12,672. We further compare BSNMF method with other six methods to semantically process co-author networks of Chinese periodicals. We compare with CPM to complete subgraph filtering method which uses 3-clique to discover the number of complete subgraphs in the network, and the undiscovered nodes are used as independent nodes to calculate the overall modularity.

Combined with the generated cooperative network, the author compares the modularity results of existing community detection methods. BSNMF program sets the initial community number as one fifth of the total number of nodes,

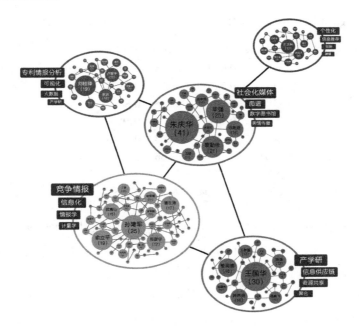

Fig. 3. Semantic co-author community discovered as knowledge graph network.

sets the superparameters $a = 5$, $b = 2$, and runs $n_{iter} = 500$ iterations to ensure convergence. In the obtained matrix S, the corresponding non-zero column has 702 columns, that is, it is divided into 702 communities. As methods 2, 5 and 6 require the initial setting of community number, the experiment is set as the community number 702 obtained by BSNMF method.

Comparing experient results in existing algorithms in Table 2, GMO algorithm has achieved a good result for community detection, and the results of community BSNMF program found modularity value is 0.9664, the highest network partition effect. At the same time, compared with the method of 5 and 6, BSNMF has achieved best experimental results.

As shown in Fig. 3, different communities obtained by the algorithm BSNMF are distinguished by different colors and area sizes, where the corresponding value of the author represents the number of the author's publication in the network. We add the title subject information in these information science journals in different community with community detection result. We can see main keywords appear of each community larger, and different communities respectively represent various professional research direction in the area of library and information science, such as "competitive intelligence", "social media", "information supply chain" and "patent intelligence" on different knowledge topics. By adding semantic information to the community detection results, the degree of difference between different communities can be more intuitively displayed, and the semantic features of different interest communities can be mined.

6   Conclusion

The cross-application with different disciplines can greatly promote the continuous development of knowledge graph technology. Many research methods and results have been formed in the research of network quantitative analysis and community detection.

Whether it can be effectively combined with the application of knowledge graph in knowledge engineering, especially in the field of scientific and information area, and improve the search, discovery and collaboration of knowledge, needs to be further expanded by researchers.

Acknowledgments. This work was supported by NSFC (Grant No. 61772330), China Next Generation Internet IPv6 project (Grant No. NGII20170609), and the Social Science Planning of Shanghai (Grant No. 2018BTQ002).

References

1. Knowledge graph development report (2018). http://cips-upload.bj.bcebos.com/KGDevReport2018.pdf
2. Aggarwal, C.C.: Social Network Data Analytics. Springer, New York (2011). https://doi.org/10.1007/978-1-4419-8462-3
3. Bales, M.E., Johnson, S.B.: Graph theoretic modeling of large-scale semantic networks. J. Biomed. Inform. **39**(4), 451–464 (2006)
4. Bhatt, S., et al.: Knowledge graph enhanced community detection and characterization. In: Proceedings of the Twelfth ACM International Conference on Web Search and Data Mining, pp. 51–59. ACM (2019)
5. Blondel, V.D., Guillaume, J.L., Lambiotte, R., Lefebvre, E.: Fast unfolding of communities in large networks. J. Stat. Mech. Theory Exp. **2008**(10), P10008 (2008)
6. Cai, D., He, X., Han, J., Huang, T.: Graph regularized nonnegative matrix factorization for data representation. IEEE Trans. Pattern Anal. Mach. Intell. **33**(8), 1548–1560 (2011)
7. Cemgil, A.T.: Bayesian inference for nonnegative matrix factorisation models. Comput. Intell. Neurosci. **2009**, 1–17 (2009). https://doi.org/10.1155/2009/785152
8. Corominas-Murtra, B., Valverde, S., Solé, R.: The ontogeny of scale-free syntax networks: phase transitions in early language acquisition. Adv. Complex Syst. **12**(03), 371–392 (2009)
9. Council, N.R.: Network Science. The National Academies Press, Washington, DC (2005). https://doi.org/10.17226/11516, https://www.nap.edu/catalog/11516/network-science
10. Danon, L., Díaz-Guilera, A., Arenas, A.: The effect of size heterogeneity on community identification in complex networks. J. Stat. Mech. Theory Exp. **2006**(11), P11010 (2006)
11. Erétéo, G., Gandon, F., Buffa, M.: SemTagP: semantic community detection in folksonomies. In: Proceedings of the 2011 IEEE/WIC/ACM International Conferences on Web Intelligence and Intelligent Agent Technology, vol. 01, pp. 324–331. IEEE Computer Society (2011)
12. Fevotte, C., Idier, J.: Algorithms for nonnegative matrix factorization with the beta-divergence. Neural Comput. **23**(9), 2421–2456 (2011)

13. Han, X., Chen, D., Yang, H.: A semantic community detection algorithm based on quantizing progress. Complexity **2019**, 13 (2019)
14. Henk, V., Vahdati, S., Nayyeri, M., Ali, M., Yazdi, H.S., Lehmann, J.: Metaresearch recommendations using knowledge graph embeddings (2019)
15. Ji, G., He, S., Xu, L., Liu, K., Zhao, J.: Knowledge graph embedding via dynamic mapping matrix. In: Proceedings of the 53rd Annual Meeting of the Association for Computational Linguistics and the 7th International Joint Conference on Natural Language Processing (Volume 1: Long Papers), vol. 1, pp. 687–696 (2015)
16. Juanzi, L., Lei, H.: Review of knowledge graph research. J. ShanXi Univ. (Nat. Aci. Ed.) **40**(03), 454–459 (2017)
17. Kianian, S., Khayyambashi, M.R., Movahhedinia, N.: Semantic community detection using label propagation algorithm. J. Inf. Sci. **42**(2), 166–178 (2016)
18. Lai, D., Wu, X., Lu, H., Nardini, C.: Learning overlapping communities in complex networks via non-negative matrix factorization. Int. J. Mod. Phys. C **22**(10), 1173–1190 (2011)
19. Lancichinetti, A., Fortunato, S.: Community detection algorithms: a comparative analysis. Phys. Rev. E **80**(5), 056117 (2009)
20. Le Martelot, E., Hankin, C.: Fast multi-scale detection of relevant communities in large-scale networks. Comput. J. **56**(9), 1136–1150 (2013)
21. Li, M., Lee, W.C., Sivasubramaniam, A.: Semantic small world: an overlay network for peer-to-peer search. In: Proceedings of the 12th IEEE International Conference on Network Protocols, ICNP 2004, pp. 228–238. IEEE (2004)
22. Lu, H., Fu, Z., Shu, X.: Non-negative and sparse spectral clustering. Pattern Recognit. **47**(1), 418–426 (2014)
23. Martinez-Rodriguez, J.L., Lopez-Arevalo, I., Rios-Alvarado, A.B., Li, X.: A brief comparison of community detection algorithms over semantic web data. In: ISWLOD@ IBERAMIA, pp. 34–44 (2016)
24. Newman, M.E.: Modularity and community structure in networks. Proc. Natl. Acad. Sci. **103**(23), 8577–8582 (2006)
25. Pastor-Satorras, R., Vespignani, A.: Epidemic spreading in scale-free networks. Phys. Rev. Lett. **86**(14), 3200 (2001)
26. Paulheim, H.: Machine learning with and for semantic web knowledge graphs. In: d'Amato, C., Theobald, M. (eds.) Reasoning Web 2018. LNCS, vol. 11078, pp. 110–141. Springer, Cham (2018). https://doi.org/10.1007/978-3-030-00338-8_5
27. Qi, W., Fucai, C., Ruiyang, H., Zhengchaos, C.: Community detection in heterogeneous network with semantic paths. Acta Electron. Sin. **6**, 030 (2016)
28. Qiao, L., Yang, L., Hong, D., Yao, L., et al.: Knowledge graph construction techniques. J. Comput. Res. Dev. **53**(3), 582–600 (2016)
29. Rörden, J., Revenko, A., Haslhofer, B., Blumauer, A.: Network-based knowledge graph assessment. In: Proceedings of the Posters and Demos Track of the 13th International Conference on Semantic Systems - SEMANTiCS 2017 (2017)
30. Schmidt, M.N., Laurberg, H.: Nonnegative matrix factorization with gaussian process priors. Comput. Intell. Neurosci. **2008**, 3 (2008)
31. Shi, X., Lu, H., He, Y., He, S.: Community detection in social network with pairwisely constrained symmetric non-negative matrix factorization. In: Proceedings of the 2015 IEEE/ACM International Conference on Advances in Social Networks Analysis and Mining 2015, ASONAM 2015, pp. 541–546. ACM, New York (2015)
32. Steyvers, M., Tenenbaum, J.B.: The large-scale structure of semantic networks: statistical analyses and a model of semantic growth. Cogn. Sci. **29**(1), 41–78 (2005)

33. Stokman, F.N., de Vries, P.H.: Structuring knowledge in a graph. In: van der Veer, G.C., Mulder, G. (eds.) Human-Computer Interaction, pp. 186–206. Springer, Heidelberg (1988). https://doi.org/10.1007/978-3-642-73402-1_12

34. Tang, L., Liu, H.: Community detection and mining in social media. Synth. Lect. Data Min. Knowl. Discov. **2**(1), 1–137 (2010)

35. Thompson, G.W., Kello, C.: Walking across wikipedia: a scale-free network model of semantic memory retrieval. Front. Psychol. **5**, 86 (2014)

36. Travers, J., Milgram, S.: The small world problem. Phychol. Today **1**(1), 61–67 (1967)

37. Wang, F., Li, T., Wang, X., Zhu, S., Ding, C.: Community discovery using non-negative matrix factorization. Data Min. Knowl. Discov. **22**(3), 493–521 (2011)

38. Xia, Z., Bu, Z.: Community detection based on a semantic network. Knowl. Based Syst. **26**, 30–39 (2012)

39. Xiaohua, S., Hongtao, L.: Research of community detection in scientific cooperation network with Bayesian NMF. Data Anal. Knowl. Disc. **1**(09), 49–56 (2017)

40. Xu, W., Liu, X., Gong, Y.: Document clustering based on non-negative matrix factorization. In: Proceedings of the 26th Annual International ACM SIGIR Conference on Research and Development in Information Retrieval, pp. 267–273. ACM (2003)

41. Yang, C., Liu, Z., Zhao, D., Sun, M., Chang, E.: Network representation learning with rich text information. In: Twenty-Fourth International Joint Conference on Artificial Intelligence (2015)

42. Yang, J., Leskovec, J.: Overlapping community detection at scale: a nonnegative matrix factorization approach. In: Proceedings of the Sixth ACM International Conference on Web Search and Data Mining, pp. 587–596. ACM (2013)

43. Yang, J., Leskovec, J.: Defining and evaluating network communities based on ground-truth. Knowl. Inf. Syst. **42**(1), 181–213 (2015)

44. Yu, X., Jing, Y., Zhiqiang, X.: A semantic overlapping community detecting algorithm in social network based on random walk. J. Comput. Res. Dev. **52**(2), 499–511 (2015)

45. Zhang, H.: The scale-free nature of semantic web ontology. In: Proceedings of the 17th International Conference on World Wide Web, pp. 1047–1048. ACM (2008)

A Survey of Relation Extraction
of Knowledge Graphs

Aoran Li[1], Xinmeng Wang[1], Wenhuan Wang[1], Anman Zhang,
and Bohan Li[1,2(✉)]

[1] College of Computer Science and Technology,
Nanjing University of Aeronautics and Astronautics,
No. 29 Jiangjun Ave, Jiangning District, Nanjing 211106, Jiangsu, China
bhli@nuaa.edu.cn
[2] Collaborative Innovation Center of Novel Software Technology
and Industrialization, Nanjing 210016, Jiangsu, China

Abstract. With the widespread use of big data, knowledge graph has become a new hotspot. It is used in intelligent question answering, recommendation system, map navigation and so on. Constructing a knowledge graph includes ontology construction, annotated data, relation extraction, and ontology inspection. Relation extraction is to solve the problem of entity semantic linking, which is of great significance to many natural language processing applications. Research related to relation extraction has gained momentum in recent years, necessitating a comprehensive survey to offer a bird's-eye view of the current state of relation extraction. In this paper, we discuss the development process of relation extraction, and classify the relation extraction algorithms in recent years. Furthermore, we discuss deep learning, reinforcement learning, active learning and transfer learning. By analyzing the basic principles of supervised learning, unsupervised learning, semi-supervised learning and distant supervision, we elucidate the characteristics of different relation extraction algorithms, and give the potential research directions in the future.

Keywords: Knowledge graph · Relation extraction · Machine learning

1 Introduction[1]

1.1 Knowledge Graph

Knowledge graphs are playing an important role in the transition of big data. We know that knowledge graphs are semantically linked entities, which translate people's cognition of the physical world into semantic information that can be understood by computers in a structured way. The extensive application of knowledge graph makes it develop to intelligence continuously. In recent years, as knowledge graph has become a hot topic in academic and busines. Cn-DBpedia [1] and zhishi.me [2] have successively

---

[1] The Science Foundation for Youth Science and Technology Innovation of Nanjing University of Aeronautics and Astronautics under Grant NJ20160028, NT2018028, NS2018057.

J. Song and X. Zhu (Eds.): APWeb-WAIM 2019 Workshops, LNCS 11809, pp. 52–66, 2019.
https://doi.org/10.1007/978-3-030-33982-1_5

emerged Chinese knowledge graph models based on relation extraction. As a large-scale semantic knowledge base, entities and relationships are the key elements of knowledge graphs. Knowledge graphs classify and integrate internet data into simple and clear triple expression forms and store them in databases. Figure 1 is the directed relation graph of the knowledge graph triplet. Most of the description languages it uses are ontology languages developed, such as RDFS [3] language, OWL [4] language and so on. Entities are connected with each other through relationships to form a network of knowledge structure [5]. Figure 2 is an example of a knowledge graph relationship. Figure 3 shows a conceptual evolution graph of knowledge graphs.

Fig. 1. A directed graph of relation triple

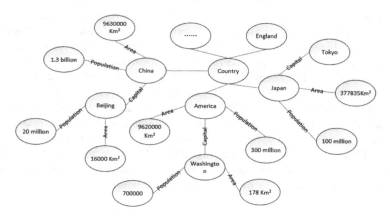

Fig. 2. An example of knowledge graph relationship

The entity includes country and city, and the attribute includes population and area. An example of (entity, relationship, entity) is (Japan - capital - Tokyo). A concrete expression for (entity - attribute - attribute) value is (Japan - population - 100 million).

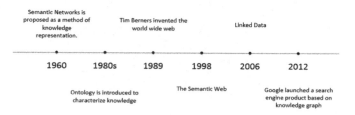

Fig. 3. Conceptual evolution graph of knowledge graphs

1.2   Related Work

At present, knowledge graphs are used in many fields, such as question answering system, expert system, database, recommendation system, intelligent medical treatment and so on. Figure 4 shows some application areas of knowledge graphs. For example, Zhang et al. [6] changed the traditional research method based on semantic analysis and designed a Q&A system of knowledge graph based on information extraction and deep learning. Although they solved the problem of low accuracy of traditional models in entity recognition, they still could not meet the needs of complex Q&A in specific applications.

In recent years, entity extraction has become more and more applied, making more and more scholars devote themselves to research relation extraction. Since 1998, the concept of relation extraction was first proposed in the important meeting of MUC [7], and the concept of relation extraction is widely used in various fields. Knowledge extraction is the main task of the knowledge graph, which is of great significance to the understanding of semantic. Some traditional knowledge extraction techniques and methods cannot well adapt to the large-scale and big data information extraction system. To solve the above problems, the concept of open information extraction is proposed. In terms of technical means, knowledge extraction develops rapidly from manual extraction stage to a statistical method based on data corpus, and then to open information extraction technology. For example, the YAGO [8] model USES Word-Net to extract entity relationships from large-scale knowledge bases with an accuracy of 97%. BANKO M et al. introduced a new OIE model framework, which makes up for the high cost of data analysis in traditional information extraction systems [9]. In 2014, Yang et al. further improved the low extraction performance of YAGO model [10]. In addition, KnowItAll [11], TextRunner [12, 13], WOE [14], ReVerb [15], R2A2 [16] and other systems promoted the development of binary relation extraction and n-element relation extraction in relation extraction under open environment.

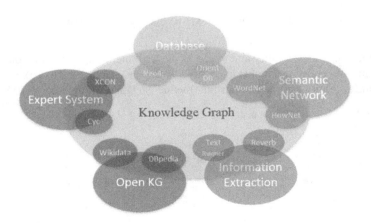

Fig. 4. Examples of knowledge graphs

1.3   Organization Structure

This paper is organized as follows. The first section introduces the basic concept and related work of knowledge graphs. Section 2 introduces common algorithms in relation extraction. Figure 5 is a flow chart of relation extraction. Figure 6 shows the evolution process of relation extraction. The third section describes the development process of the latest unsupervised algorithm. Section 4 introduces the development of supervised algorithm in detail and we sort out some popular semi-supervised algorithms in Sect. 5. Section 6 introduces the development status of distant supervision. Finally, conclusions are made in the last section.

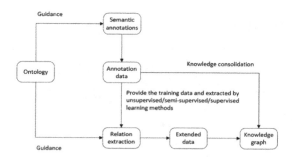

Fig. 5.   Relation extraction flow chart

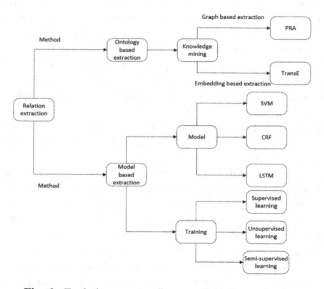

Fig. 6.   Evolution process diagram of relation extraction

2   Relation Extraction Algorithm

As an important part of information extraction, relation extraction extracts semantic relationships among entities by identifying their relationships. In the real world, the extraction of the relation is more complicated than entity extraction, and the forms in natural sentences are diversified, so the extraction of the relation is more difficult than entity extraction. How to extract the relationship between entities in real-world data efficiently is the focus of current knowledge graph information extraction (Fig. 7).

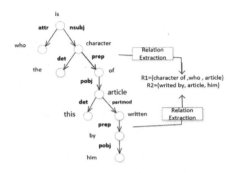

Fig. 7. Extracting instances of syntax components for a tree diagram

The relationships in the syntactic tree include "character of" and "written by". Since "article" and side 'pobj' are connected with the preposition "of", it is concluded that the object of "character of" is entity "article". The closest word to "character of" is "who", so it is the subject of "character of".

In the common relation extraction algorithms, pattern matching and dictionary driving require experts with professional skills to build a large-scale knowledge base and make rules manually, which is time-consuming and laborious, inefficient and poor in portability [17]. In order to solve these shortcomings, methods based on machine learning are generated. At present, the relation extraction method based on machine learning has been widely used in various fields. This method treats the extraction of relation as a simple classification problem. The basic judgment is made by simple manpower, and then the classifier is constructed. The introduction of adaptive information extraction, open information extraction, and other technical means promotes the rapid development of machine learning. Relation extraction methods based on machine learning can be divided into four categories according to whether the training data are labeled or not, mainly including supervised learning, unsupervised learning, semi-supervised learning, and distant supervised learning. Table 1 is the analysis and comparison of four kinds of relation extraction algorithms based on machine learning. Table 2 is the analysis and comparison of classical relation extraction algorithms in machine learning.

Machine learning has also undergone four important periods: Deep Learning, Reinforcement Learning, Transfer Learning, and Active Learning. The birth of the corresponding algorithm has also made a great contribution to the improvement of machine learning performance and scalability, making the scope of application of machine learning more and more. The active learning algorithm is the frontier field of machine learning and relation extraction. It is a learning method suitable for small data and non-label data occupying large scenes and is often applied in a semi-supervised or weakly supervised environment, together with Transfer Learning. For example, Denis Gudovskiy and Alec Hodgkinson proposed an EBA attention mechanism combining deep learning and active learning based on the latest DNNS method [18], which improved the accuracy of feature extraction of MNIST and SVHN data sets and achieved great results. Deep learning is often combined with reinforcement learning to become deep reinforcement learning. For example, in 2019, Wang et al. designed a new neural network structure that is no model [19], which has the advantage of being easy to integrate with reinforcement learning.

Table 1. Analysis and comparison of machine learning algorithms.

Name	Portability	Manual intervention	Advantages	Disadvantages
Supervised learning	Weak	Strong	Easy; The ambiguity of samples is low	Low efficiency
Semi-supervised learning	Medium	Weak	Easy to understand; High efficiency	Iteration results are not stable
Unsupervised learning	Strong	Weak	Low cost; No data samples are required	The ambiguity of samples is high; Low accuracy

Table 2. Analysis and comparison of classical relation extraction algorithms.

Type	Classic algorithms	Advantages	Disadvantages
Unsupervised learning	LDA	Low cost; Unlabeled data	Unreliable accuracy; Uncontrolled
Supervised learning	SVM	Good generalization ability	Low efficiency; Sensitive to missing data
	Logistic regression	Easy to adjust; High rate of prediction	Underfit; only deal with binary classification
Semi-supervised learning	Bootstrapping	Reduce the amount of annotated data used	Not applicable to network-level data
	Cooperative training	Easy to understand; Stable; Fast convergent	The vote does not determine the credibility of the mark
	Standard Propagation	Simple; High efficiency; unlimited	Iteration results are unstable; Low accuracy

3 Unsupervised Learning

Unsupervised Learning does not need to have the label data, can intelligently extract the entity relations of the data. The simple goal of unsupervised learning is to build a base class model from the data and train the algorithm to generate its own data instance. Since the training data has no label, it can make up for the deficiency in manual extraction relation and has the characteristics of strong adaptability and high efficiency. Unsupervised relation extraction algorithm was first proposed by Hasegawa in 2004 [20], in which he proposed a named entity relation extraction method based on misdirected. Since then, many unsupervised algorithms have improved on this approach.

In 2013, Socher, Chen et al. [21] aiming at the lack of reasoning ability of discrete entities and relationships in a knowledge base, proposed an expressive neural tensor networks model suitable for the reasoning of two-entity relationships, further proving the applicability of unsupervised learning algorithm. They reproduced the methods of Bordes et al. [22] and Jenatton et al. [23], and improved and optimized them on the basis of this method, so as to prove that when word vectors are initialized into learning vectors in the unsupervised corpus, the accuracy of relevant models established will be higher. Traditional unsupervised learning is basically a clustering algorithm, and most of these learning methods are based on statistical methods and have no feedback ability. Therefore, Heck et al. combined the statistical method of the deep semantic method of AI community and proposed an unsupervised semantic analysis learning algorithm based on large-scale semantic knowledge graph, which does not need semantic pattern design, data collection or manual annotation [24]. In addition, a graph crawling algorithm for data mining is proposed. In their experiments, they combined the two methods and achieved results similar to those of semantic analyzers that monitor annotation training. In 2019, Luus and others skillfully combined unsupervised algorithms with interactive transfer learning algorithms and active learning tools [25]. They selected images of 1000 labels as data sets for feature information extraction. On the basis of CNN, by reducing the dimensions of the semi-supervised t-SNE algorithm model, using the interactive transfer learning method and the low complexity active learning tool, the effect of significantly improving the marking efficiency is achieved.

4 Supervised Learning

The supervised relation extraction algorithm is a relatively perfect system. Supervised relation extraction can be divided into eigenvector-based method and kernel function-based method [26]. Xia [27] proposed a feature-based Chinese term relation extraction method based on a naive bayesian algorithm and perceptron algorithm. Considering the dependency relationship, the position of features was added to the vector space model to form a new feature representation method. In addition, support vector machine (SVM) [28], Winnow [29] and so on all construct classifiers based on feature vector learning. The method based on sum function does not need to construct eigenvector space, and its processing object is a structure tree, which improves the shortcoming of the eigenvector. Because supervised learning algorithms are limited by the availability of training corpus, they cannot identify special semantic relationships and are not suitable for large-scale data. In recent years, as large-scale knowledge bases such as Wikipedia and Freebase keep emerging, in order to further expand the scale, it is necessary to study new methods of constructing knowledge graphs. Therefore, Dong et al. [30] proposed a method of how to build a knowledge base of network scale in 2014. The knowledgebase system constructed by them has high accuracy in checking the facts.

5   Semi-supervised Learning

5.1   Co-Training Algorithm

After Blum and Mitchell proposed the Co-Training algorithm in 1998, the Co-Training algorithm becomes one of the most important parts in the semi-supervised learning field due to its characteristics of easy understanding, stability and fast convergence [31]. It catches widespread attention from many scholars and has achieved many research results. The Self-Training algorithm is one of the first algorithms proposed to use unlabeled data [32]. The main idea of the algorithm is to train the classifier with the labeled data set, and classify the classifier according to the training. According to the trained classifier, some reliable unlabeled data is marked and added to the labeled data set to form a new labeled data set. Iterate over and stop training when the labeled data set reaches the predetermined requirement. The biggest contribution of the Self-Training algorithm to the Co-Training algorithm is that it first proposed the idea of training the classifier with unlabeled data, which laid the ideological foundation for the future algorithms. The Co-Training algorithm is a new algorithm based on the Self-Training algorithm. This algorithm requires more than one redundant view of the data attributes. By cooperatively training two different classifiers A and B, the classifier produces the result and then cross joins another classifier different from it. That is to say, the labeled results obtained by classifier A should be added to the data set of classifier B, and the labeled results obtained by classifier B should be added to the data set of classifier A. According to the above process, the labeled results can be obtained by multiple analysis from two classifiers. In some special cases, the Co-Training algorithm is completely equivalent to the self-training algorithm.

However, in most cases, it is difficult for the data set to meet the requirements of more than one redundant view. The Co-Training algorithm will have errors when processing this data set, which needs further improvement and modification [33]. Therefore, in 2005, Zhou and Li proposed the Tri-Training algorithm [34], which relaxed the constraints on the data set. The algorithm extends the independence between neural networks participating in collaborative training. To a certain extent, it solves the problem that co-training algorithm is limited in performance improvement. The classification accuracy of the neural network is improved, and the performance of the cooperative training algorithm is also improved. In 2007, Zhou and Li further refined the Tri-Training algorithm and proposed the Co-Forest algorithm [35]. The Co-Forest algorithm breaks the constraint on using two classifiers and switches to n different classifiers. Therefore, compared with Tri-Training algorithm, Co-Forest algorithm plays a better role in inheritance learning and has good robustness. In 2011,

Zhou and Zhang proposed the Co-Trade algorithm [36]. The Co-Trade algorithm makes full use of the marked data in the noiseless environment. However, the Co-Trade algorithm cannot use simple voting to determine the credibility of the mark. Table 3 shows the advantages and disadvantages of various Co-Training algorithms. With the continuous improvement of Co-Training algorithms, applications based on Co-Training algorithms gradually penetrate into many fields, such as natural language processing, image retrieval and pattern recognition.

Table 3. Comparison of Co-Training algorithms.

Name	Algorithm time	Advantages	Disadvantages
Self-Training	1990s	Easy to understand; Easy; More basic	Some limitations; Low accuracy
Co-Training	2000s	More accuracy; More stable	Some limitations; Low efficiency
Tri-Training	2005	Better performance; Improved classification accuracy	Have to use two classifiers
Co-Forest	2007	Good robustness; Have N classifiers	Use more markup data
Co-Trade	2011	Use less markup data	Complex

5.2 MULTIR Algorithm

Semi-supervision is a promising approach that can be scaled up to deal with different relationships [37]. Based on the semi-supervised knowledge graph, it is possible to extract a large number of potential quantitative relations by using structured labeled data. Many of the earlier semi-supervised methods assume that two relationships do not allow the same argument. In order to solve such problems, the MULTIR algorithm is proposed. MULTIR is a semi-supervised model of multi-instance learning that deals with overlapping relationships and aims to provide a joint approach [37]. This algorithm can automatically generate the relational extractor and mark the training corpus. The main algorithm of the model is to combine the simple corpus and the sentence-level extraction model to generate more accurate sentence-level predictions, then decode each individual sentence, aggregate individual facts, and perform corpus-level extraction. According to the relevant experiments, the MULTIR algorithm model can be run very quickly in terms of the overall corpus and sentence extraction methods. In recent years, more and more scholars have participated in semi-supervised research. In 2018, Li et al. applied the GCN model of machine learning in semi-supervised learning [38]. In 2019, Luan et al. proposed a general framework DYGIE [39] for dynamic span map information extraction. Agrawal et al. extracted a related structured information on a large number of existing original scientific literatures and proposed a new, scalable, semi-supervised method [40]. Semi-supervised algorithms are becoming the research direction of more and more scholars. Table 4 shows the process of generating relational data from natural language text.

Table 4. Examples of information extraction.

Data A	Data B	Basic tuples	Sentence	Conclusion
Jobs	Apple	Founded (Jobs, Apple)	S1 = "Steve Jobs founded apple, inc."	S may be the natural language expression of the facts held by r (e1, e2), or it could be a useful training example
Newton	Apple	Through (Newton, Apple)	S2 = "Newton discovered gravity through the apple."	
Amy	Jack	Teach (Amy, Jack)	S3 = "Amy is Jack's English teacher."	
July	Sam	Birth (July, Sam)	S4 = "Sam's birthday is in July."	

5.3 Scientific Paper Extraction Algorithm

Compared with general papers, scientific information papers contain a large amount of academic terms and expertise, which requires researchers to have basic knowledge and knowledge in this area. However, in the face of a large number of documents containing scientific information, manual extraction of structured information from these documents is inefficient, resource utilization is low, and annotation costs are high. Therefore, how to extract the overall structure and summary information of an paper in a large number of documents becomes an urgent problem to be solved. Since 2010, Kim [41], Gollapalli [42], Jaidka [43] and others systematically extracted scientific literature through unsupervised learning methods. But unsupervised learning has certain limitations on unlabeled data. Therefore, in 2019, Agrawal et al. proposed a novel, scalable, domain-independent, semi-supervised scientific paper extraction algorithm [44]. The main idea of the algorithm is to extract the words of the core vocabulary in the literature through semi-supervised methods, and further obtain related concept phrases such as methods and results in the literature. Case studies in the fields of computational linguistics and computer vision show that the algorithm has strong regional independence, high system recall and precision, and statistically significant improvements. By using this algorithm, we can construct and extract knowledge graphs of scientific documents efficiently and accurately, and make up for the deficiency of unsupervised learning methods in structured extraction.

5.4 Active Learning

Recently, some modified algorithms combine active learning with semi-supervision. Thomas Drugman, Janne Pylkkonen and others even applied active learning and semi-supervised training in the field of speech recognition [45]. In addition to the wide range of applications in image feature extraction and speech recognition, active learning can also be applied to the field of natural language processing (NLP). In 2019, Arora et al.

developed an active learning method for filtering natural language information and extracting domain models [46]. Their method is calculated to be as high as 96% due to the use of active learning. To further improve the accuracy of identifying natural language elements, they are studying how to improve the transfer learning algorithm and apply it to the extraction domain model.

6 Distant Supervised Learning

Distant Supervision was first proposed by Mintz [47] and others at ACL2009. Because of the high cost and limited number of labeled training data in supervised algorithms, purely unsupervised methods can use large amounts of data and extract relationships, but the resulting relationships are not easily labeled to the relationships required for a particular knowledge base. Therefore, they combined the advantages of supervision and unsupervised, and proposed the distant supervision relation extraction. It also proves the role of syntactic features in the information extraction of long-distance supervision. In 2015, Daojian Zeng, Kang Liu and others discovered that there are two types of problems in distant supervision relation extraction. One type is that heuristic text alignment may cause label errors; the other is due to the limitations of the application scope of traditional statistical models, and the feature extraction process may be cumbersome and may cause unknown errors. In 2012, Surdeanu et al. [48] proposed the distant supervision hypothesis of "multi-instance learning". In 2014, Zeng, Lai et al. [49] used convolutional deep neural network to extract lexical and sentence hierarchical features. Inspired by them, Zeng et al. borrowed the above-mentioned "multi-instance learning" method for noise data and error labels, and trained the model with a highly confident training data set. In response to the limitations of statistical models, they also proposed a Piecewise Convolutional Neural Networks (PCNN) [50]. The model is relatively simple, and the difference from the traditional convolutional neural network is mainly due to the change of the pooling layer. Finally, they implemented a multi-instance learning PCNN to extract the long-distance super-vision relationship. The advantage of this method lies in the introduction of innovation into the multi-instance learning relation extraction task. It is proposed that the PCNNs model can get more useful information in the sentence. The disadvantage is that "multi-instance learning" will waste some useful sentence features.

   With the wide application of distant supervision, noise data and error labels are also increasing, which seriously affects the performance of relation extraction. In order to further alleviate this problem, in 2016, Yankai Lin and others improved the papers published by Daojian Zeng et al. in 2015. They believe that the "multi-example learning" method alleviates the problem of more noise data, but Since only the sample with the highest confidence in each packet is used as the training data, a lot of useful information is lost while filtering out the noise. A convolutional neural network model based on the extraction of attention mechanism is proposed [51]. In this model, CNN are used to embed the semantics of sentences, and sentence-level attention mechanisms are used to assign weights to sentences. Their experimental results show that this new model has better prediction performance and better performance than advanced feature-based methods and neural network methods. The disadvantage is that the attention mechanism needs to loop through each relationship, which is more complicated, and only uses the attention mechanism at the sentence level. The word hierarchy does not consider the attention mechanism. Guanying Wang put forward a new perspective on the cause of the mislabeling problem in 2018. They suppose that the error label of distant supervision is mainly caused by the incomplete use of knowledge graph information, so the unlabeled distant monitoring method can solve the noise label. Under the assumption that the relationship label is not used, the knowledge of the classifier is monitored using the prior knowledge of the knowledge graph [52]. Experiments show that this new method works well and its performance is better than the most advanced results in distant supervision, which can effectively solve the noise label problem. Table 5 shows a general analysis and comparison of the above distant supervision algorithms.

Table 5. Analysis and comparison of several new distant Supervision algorithms.

Method name	Time	Advantages	Disadvantages	Author
Mintz	2009	Low cost; Suitable for large data size	Limited; Wrong label	Mike Mintz
Multi-Instance	2012	Avoid missing values; Handle mixed predictions	Low efficiency	Mihai Surdeanu
Convolutional deep neural network	2014	Simple pre-processing; Improved efficiency	Wrong label	Daojian Zeng; Siwei Lai
PCNN	2015	The Wrong label resolved; Feature extraction error solved	Wasted sentences' Characteristics	Daojian Zeng; Yubo Chen
Attention	2016	Better prediction	High complexity; Unconsidered word layers	Yankai Lin; Shiqi Shen

7   Conclusion

Recently, with the increasing popularity of artificial intelligence, big data and block-chain, knowledge graph has played an important role in different areas. A large number of applications based on deep learning and basic model algorithms emerge. In this paper, the relation extraction algorithms of existing knowledge graphs are analyzed and compared, and some popular relation extraction algorithms and current research status are introduced. The advantages and disadvantages of the four types of machine learning algorithms are detailed, and their algorithm ideas and development history are expounded respectively. Community detection research, embedding models, intelligent answer system are becoming hot topics and important research areas in complex network fields. Not only can we analyze communities in the knowledge distribution and evolution trajectory detection domains, but also explore the knowledge diagrams of a unified embedded model. Definitely, knowledge graph will enter a bigger picture in the future.

References

1. Xu, B., et al.: CN-DBpedia: a never-ending chinese knowledge extraction system. In: Benferhat, S., Tabia, K., Ali, M. (eds.) IEA/AIE 2017. LNCS (LNAI), vol. 10351, pp. 428–438. Springer, Cham (2017). https://doi.org/10.1007/978-3-319-60045-1_44
2. Niu, X., Sun, X.R., Wang, H.F., et al.: Zhishi.meweaving Chinese linking open data. In: Proceedings of the 10th International Semantic Web Conference, Bonn, Germany, pp. 205–220 (2011)
3. Pan, J.Z., Horrocks, I.: RDFS(FA): connecting RDF(S) and OWL DL. IEEE Trans. Knowl. Data Eng. 19(2), 192–206 (2007). https://doi.org/10.1109/TKDE.2007.37
4. Mcguiness, D.L., Harmelen, F.: OWL Web ontology language overview. W3C Recomm. 63(45), 990–996 (2004)
5. Qiao, L., Yang, L., Hong, D., et al.: Knowledge graph construction techniques. J. Comput. Res. Dev. 53(3), 582–600 (2016). (in Chinese)
6. Zhang, C., Chang, L., Wang, W., Chen, H., Bin, C.: Question and answer over fine-grained knowledge graph based on BiLSTM-CRF (2019)
7. Proceedings of the 6th Message Understanding Conference (MUC - 7). National Institute of Standars and Technology (1998)
8. Suchanek, F.M., Kasneci, G., Weikum, G.: YAGO: a core of semantic knowledge unifying WordNet and Wikipedia. In: Proceedings of WWW (2007)
9. Banko, M., Cafarella, M.J., Soderland, S., et al.: Open information extraction for the web. In: Proceedings of the 20th Int Joint Conf on Artificial Intelligence, pp. 2670–2676. ACM, New York (2007)
10. Yang, B., Cai, D.-F., Yang, H.: Progress in open information extraction. J. Chin. Inf. Process. 4, 1–11 (2014)
11. Etzioni, O., Cafarella, M., Downey, D., et al.: Unsupervised named-entity extraction from the web: an experimental study. Artif. Intell. 165(1), 91–134 (2005)
12. Banko, M., Cafarella, M.J., Soderland, S., et al.: Open information extraction from the web. In: Proceedings of IJCAI (2007)
13. Banko, M., Etzioni, O.: The tradeoffs between open and traditional relation extraction. In: Proceedings of Annual Meeting of the Association for Computational Linguistics (2008)
14. Wu, F., Weld, D.S.: Open information extraction using Wikipedia. In: Proceedings of Annual Meeting of the Association for Computational Linguistics, pp. 118–127 (2010)
15. Fader, A., Soderland, S., Etzioni, O.: Identifying relations for open information extraction. In: Proceedings of Conference on Empirical Methods in Natural Language Processing (2011)
16. Etzioni, O., Fader, A., Christensen, J., et al.: Open information extraction: the second generation. In: Proceedings of International Joint Conference on Artificial Intelligence (2011)
17. Xu, J., Zhang, Z., Wu, Z.: Review on techniques of entity relation extraction. New Technol. Libr. Inf. Serv. 168(8), 18–23 (2008)
18. Gudovskiy, D., Hodgkinson, A.: Explanation-based attention for semi-supervised deep active learning (2019)

19. Wang, Z., Schaul, T., Hessel, M., van Hasselt, H., Lanctot, M.: Dueling network architectures for deep reinforcement learning (2019)
20. Hasegawa, T., Sekine, S., Grishman, R.: Discovering relations among named entities from large corpora. In: Proceedings of ACL-2004, pp. 415–422 (2004)
21. Socher, R., Chen, D., Manning, C.D., Ng, A.Y.: Reasoning with neural tensor networks for knowledge base completion (2013)
22. Bordes, A., Weston, J., Collobert, R., Bengio, Y.: Learning structured embeddings of knowledge bases. In: AAAI (2011)
23. Jenatton, R., Le Roux, N., Bordes, A., Obozinski, G.: A latent factor model for highly multi-relational data. In: NIPS (2012)
24. Heck, L., Hakkani-Tür, D., Tur, G.: Leveraging knowledge graphs for web-scale unsupervised semantic parsing. In: ISCA (2013)
25. Luus, F., Khan, N., Akhalwaya, I.: Active learning with TensorBoard projector (2019)
26. Liu, F., Zhong, Z., Lei, L., Wu, Y.: Entity relation extraction method based on machine learning (2013)
27. Xia, S., Lehong, D.: Feature-based approach to Chinese term relation extraction In: 2009 International Conference on Signal Processing Systems, pp. 410–414 (2009)
28. Cristianini, N., Shawe-Taylor, J.: An Introduction to Support Vector Machines. Cambridge University Press, Cambridge University (2000)
29. Zhang, T.: Regularized winnow methods. In: Advances in Neural Information Processing Systems 13, pp. 703–709 (2001)
30. Dong, X.L., Gabrilovich, E., Heitz, G.: Knowledge vault: a web-scale approach to probabilistic knowledge fusion. In: KDD (2014)
31. Zhou, Z.-H.: Cooperative Training Style in Semi-Supervised Learning. Machine Learning and Its Applications, pp. 259–275. Tsinghua University Press, Beijing (2007)
32. Chapelle, O., Schölkopf, B., Zien, A. (eds.): Semi-Supervised Learning (2006). The MIT Press, Cambridge
33. Pise, N.N., Kulkarni, P.: A survey of semi-supervised learning methods. In: 2008 International Conference on Computational Intelligence and Security (2008)
34. Zhou, Z.-H., Li, M.: Tri-training: exploiting unlabeled data using three classifiers. IEEE Trans. Knowl. Data Eng. 17(11), 1529–1541 (2005)
35. Li, M., Zhou, Z.-H.: Improve computer-aided diagnosis with machine learning techniques using undiagnosed samples. IEEE Trans. Syst. 19(11), 1479–1493 (2007)
36. Zhang, M.-L., Zhou, Z.-H.: CoTRADE: confident co-training with data editing. IEEE Trans. Syst. Man Cybern. Part B Cybern. 41, 1612–1626 (2011)
37. Hoffmann, R., Zhang, C., Ling, X., Zettlemoyer, L., Weld, D.S.: CoTRADE: knowledge-based weak supervision for information extraction of overlapping relations. In: The 49th Annual Meeting of the Association for Computational Linguistics: Human Language Technologies, pp. 541–550 (2011)
38. Li, Q., Han, Z., Wu, X.-M.: CoTRADE: deeper insights into graph convolutional networks for semi-supervised learning. In: The Thirty-Second AAAI Conference on Artificial Intelligence (AAAI-18) (2018)
39. Luan, Y., Wadden, D., He, L., Shah, A., Ostendorf, M., Hajishirzi, H.: CoTRADE: a general framework for information extraction using dynamic span graphs. In: NAACL (2019)
40. Agrawal, K., Mittal, A., Pudi, V.: CoTRADE: scalable, semi-supervised extraction of structured information from scientific literature, pp. 11–20. Association for Computational Linguistics (2019)

41. Kim, S.N., Medelyan, O., Kan, M.-Y., Baldwin, T.: SemEval-2010 task 5: automatic keyphrase extraction from scientifific articles. In: Proceedings of the 5th International Workshop on Semantic Evaluation, SemEval 2010, Stroudsburg, PA, USA, pp. 21–26. Association for Computational Linguistics (2010)
42. Gollapalli, S.D., Caragea, C.: Extracting keyphrases from research papers using citation networks. In: Proceedings of the Twenty-Eighth AAAI Conference on Artifificial Intelligence, AAAI 2014, pp. 1629–1635. AAAI Press (2014)
43. Jaidka, K., Chandrasekaran, M.K., Rustagi, S., Kan, M.-Y.: Insights from CL-SciSumm 2016: the faceted scientific document summarization shared task. Int. J. Digit. Libr. 19(2), 163–171 (2016)
44. Agrawal, K., Mittal, A., Pudi, V.: Scalable, semi-supervised extraction of structured information from scientifific literature (2019)
45. Drugman, T., Pylkkonen, J., Kneser, R.: Active and semi-supervised learning in ASR: benefits on the acoustic and language models (2019)
46. Arora, C., Sabetzadeh, M., Nejati, S., Briand, L.: An active learning approach for improving the accuracy of automated domain model extraction (2019)
47. Mintz, M., Bills, S., Snow, R., Jurafsky, D.: Distant supervision for relation extraction without labeled data, ACL 2009 (2009)
48. Surdeanu, M., Tibshirani, J., Nallapati, R., Manning, C.D.: Multi-instance multi-label learning for relation extraction. In: Proceedings of EMNLP-CoNLL, pp. 455–465 (2012)
49. Zeng, D., Liu, K., Lai, S., Zhou, G., Zhao, J.: Relation classification via convolutional deep neural network. In: Proceedings of COLING, pp. 2335–2344 (2014)
50. Zeng, D., Liu, K., Chen, Y., Zhao, J.: Distant supervision for relation extraction via piecewise convolutional neural networks (2015)
51. Lin, Y., Shen, S., Liu, Z., Luan, H., Sun, M.: Neural relation extraction with selective attention over instances (2016)
52. Wang, G., Zhang, W., Wang, R., Zhou, Y.: Label-free distant supervision for relation extraction via knowledge graph embedding (2018)

DSEA

PEVR: Pose Estimation for Vehicle Re-Identification

Saifullah Tumrani[1]([⊠]), Zhiyi Deng[1], Abdullah Aman Khan[1], and Waqar Ali[1,2]

[1] School of Computer Science and Engineering, University of Electronic Science
and Technology of China, Chengdu 611731, China
{saif.tumrani,abdkhan}@std.uestc.edu.cn, zhiyidng@gmail.com,
waqar.uestc@yahoo.com
[2] Faculty of Information Technology, The University of Lahore, Lahore, Pakistan

Abstract. Re-identification is a challenging task because the available information is partial. This paper presents an approach to tackle vehicle re-identification (Re-id) problem. We focus on pose estimation for vehicles, which is an important module of vehicle Re-id. Person Re-id received huge attention, while vehicle re-id was ignored, but recently the computer vision community have started focusing on this topic and have tried to solve this problem by only using spatiotemporal information while neglecting the driving direction. The proposed technique is using visual features to find poses of the vehicle which helps to find driving directions. Experiments are conducted on publicly available datasets VeRi and CompCars, the proposed approach got excellent results.

Keywords: Vehicle re-identification · Pose estimation · Pose classifying model · Machine learning

1 Introduction

Vehicles i.e. cars, buses, trucks, etc. are a necessary part of human life, which plays a vital role in transportation and mass transfer. Moreover, vehicles are an important object class in advanced monitoring systems having many applications such as recognition at the parking lot, automatic toll collecting on the highway, vehicle tracking and collection of traffic data. Research regarding person re-id is being conducted from the past decade. Until recently, vehicle re-id was ignored but many researchers in computer vision community are now focusing on this area. However, this area of research still holds a lot of room for future research and has many significant gaps as compared to person re-id. The previous researches focused on detection [1], segmentation [2] and classification [3]. Re-id aims to find the same vehicle (query image) in the vehicle surveillance database containing different images captured by different cameras, if the query image is found in the database, it is considered a re-id. Recent researchers focused on detection, classification, categorization and driver behavior modeling. Vehicle re-id is an exercise of matching the same vehicle's images with different non-overlapping images captured by surveillance cameras. Vehicle re-id is a very

© Springer Nature Switzerland AG 2019
J. Song and X. Zhu (Eds.): APWeb-WAIM 2019 Workshops, LNCS 11809, pp. 69–78, 2019.
https://doi.org/10.1007/978-3-030-33982-1_6

challenging task, as the difference between vehicles of the same model is negligible and the vehicle appearance may change with varying lighting conditions and views. In Fig. 1, each column shows distinct directions of vehicles with different view conditions. Thus, vehicle re-id models should be able to precisely find the inter-class and intra-class differences.

Fig. 1. The Poses in each column belongs to same vehicle, showing front, back, left and right sides of the vehicles with various viewpoints.

Vehicle re-id is different from tradition vehicle identification, it can be categorized as an instance-level object classification task. For a real-world example, it is treated as a progressive task. Suppose, if security agencies need to find a suspected vehicle in a city via surveillance video feed, appearance characteristics i.e. model, class and color are initially specified to search the vehicle. Afterward, the license plate is a significant feature for re-id and narrows down the search to identify the suspected vehicle.

In the past, vehicles were only identified by their unique license plate and license plate recognition [4–6]. However, the success ratio was low as the suspect's license plates can be occluded, removed or faked. Deep learning-based algorithms made effective contributions, to make it feasible for learning discriminating features from large datasets, which makes re-id easier based on visual

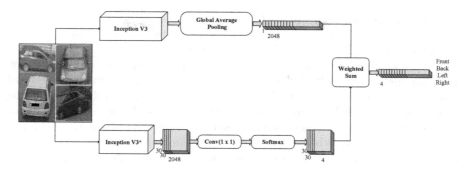

Fig. 2. PEVR framework: first our model transforms RBG images to tensor of activation through convolution backbone, while generating probability maps associated with different sides. Inception-V3* module in lower branch is modified version of Inception-V3 as stated below in inception architecture section.

appearance. However, convolution neural network (CNN) can describe certain aspects of images which may not be enough for vehicle re-id, as vehicle images have large inter-class and small intra-class variations. CNN has combined with feature extraction and metric learning recently [7,8].

As re-id is a challenging task, as similar vehicles are difficult to distinguish in real-world traffic, because of the same color, model and their spatiotemporal information are not exploited. The contributions of this paper are as follows:

1. We propose a new model to tackle important module of vehicle re-id to estimate poses of vehicles. Through a vast set of experiments, we show that our model achieves better performance than another standard deep convolutional architecture.
2. We evaluate our proposed model on two widely used public datasets VeRi [9] and CompCars [10], the efficiency of our method has been verified by related experiments.

2 Related Work

The previous researches regarding vehicle re-id can be divided based on appearance, license plate recognition, and spatiotemporal properties. The appearance of a vehicle can have high similarities such as the same color and type. Additionally, problems like occlusions, illumination variation, and multiple views make it more challenging. However, most of the work is done using visual appearance features. Some early researchers relied on various sensors other than camera, while we only rely on visual appearance of vehicle same as facial identification [11–15] or pedestrian identification [7,16,17]. Ferus *et al.* [18] used feature pool to extract appearance features of vehicles. Matei *et al.* [19] exploited kinematic and appearance constraints to track vehicle across nonoverlapping cameras. Liu *et al.* [20] proposed a model, that extracts features from local regions. As Fig. 1

shows, the same vehicle in different environments illustrates different features; methods above cannot solve the problem perfectly, due to inter-class and intra-class differences, occlusions and illumination variation.

Another concern for vehicle re-id is the license plate recognition at different places like highways, parks and parking lots. Liu *et al.* [21] proposed a method to solve the license plate recognition problem by matching the license plates to find the same vehicles by using Siamese Neural Network. Khare *et al.* [22] introduced a technique for character reconstruction to segment character of license plates based on characteristics of stroke width in laplacian and gradient domain. Hendry *et al.* [23] used You Only Look Once (YOLO) darknet deep learning framework for automatic license plate recognition. However, existing methods do not achieve good performance because of the low quality of images obtained in the open traffic environment, which makes it difficult to capture license plates. Furthermore, to improve re-id performance some researchers used spatiotemporal information obtained from camera networks.

3   Proposed Method

In this work, we verify our model using two standard deep learning architecture namely Inception V-3 [24] and ResNet [25]. We used inception-V3 [24] as the backbone for PEVR models. So, we begin to explain inception-V3 [24] architecture followed by the details for our PEVR model and then how it is integrated into our proposed framework will be described.

3.1   Inception-V3 Architecture

Inception-V3 is a deep convolutional network architecture with 48-layers. However, global average pooling is used instead of a fully-connected layer, which can operate on arbitrary input sizes. Experiments show that our model performs better than ResNet [25] with 152 layers which are 3 times more than our inception V-3. Inception V-3 is shallower and three times less computationally expensive than ResNet [25].

Inception-V3 [24], with output stride of 32, where the size of activation is reduced to $\frac{1}{8}$ of the input image resolution in the first seven layers. We used two convolutional and one max pooling layer operating on the stride size of 2 to get this reduction. Following three blocks of inception layers with two grid reduction module. In inception-V3 blocks the spatial resolution of activation is the same, the grid reduction module has half size of activation size and the number of channels is increased. Via global average polling the output of last inception module a feature vector of 2048-D. For more details, refer to [24].

3.2   Framework Overview

To make full use of local cues for vehicle re-identification, we propose Pose Estimation for Vehicle Re-Identification (PEVR) as shown in the Fig. 2. Due to pixel-level accuracy and robustness to pose variation, our model is superior.

For the appearance-based model, we adopted inception-V3 [24] as the backbone of our model. However, we made two modifications to achieve our task. The quality relies on final activation to have sufficient resolution. So, some changes are made the stride of last grid reduction in the network from 2 to 1 which results in output stride of 16 compared to original stride which is 32. To deal efficiently with extra computation, as a result, is added to the last block of inception, filters are replaced with dilated convolution filters. Global average pooling is removed and pyramid pooling is added followed by 1×1 convolution layer acting as a classifier. Which allowed us to perform pixel-level multi-class classification.

To make full use of visual cues, we use the probability maps associated with four different sides of vehicles namely; front, back, left and right. These probability maps are generated by our model and are l_1-normalized per channel. Multiple time we pooled the activation function each time with one of the four probability maps, contrasting global average pooling. Pooling activation in different regions is as weighted sum operation and the probability of weighted sum is used as weights for these poses, that results in 2048-D feature vectors each representing one side. After that to represent the sides as front, back, left and right we performed element-wise max-pooling operation followed by the results of foreground and past global representation from an image. Our technique causes the minimum computational cost to global average pooling. We believe this is a strong baseline for pose estimation for vehicle re-identification.

4 Experiments

We implemented the proposed model on VeRi [9], our experiments show that the approach effectively increases the performance of vehicle re-id by estimating the pose of vehicles.

4.1 Datasets

VeRi dataset [9] is a publically available dataset for vehicle Re-ID containing information of vehicle ID, camera ID, color, type. VeRi dataset is collected with 20 cameras and different viewpoints, occlusions, illuminations and resolutions in real-world traffic surveillance environment covering an area of $1\,Km^2$ consisting of 776 vehicles of which 576 vehicles are used for and training and remaining 200 are used for testing. There are 37778 training images while 11579 images for testing. For evaluation, each vehicle is captured from every camera is applied as query images containing 1678 images. Additionally, vehicle color and model information is also available (Table 1).

CompCars dataset [10] is a large publically available dataset containing data obtained from urban surveillance videos and network. CompCars [10] contains 136,726 partial images of different vehicle, their properties and viewpoints. We have further split the dataset and labeled the vehicles with 4 different viewpoints categorized as front, back, left and respectively. We trained our model with both of these datasets and tested on testing set of VeRi [9] dataset and manually split CompCars [10] for training and testing.

VeRi dataset [9] lacks pose labels of vehicles, by utilizing images of CompCars [10] which are labeled the vehicles viewpoints to train our model. We categories the datasets manually in four subsets as i.e. front, back, left and right from training images. We have scaled the samples to $227 * 227$ to train and test our network.

Table 1. The detail information of dataset

Dataset	VeRi	CompCars
Training Images	37778	136,726
Testing Images	11579	-
Number of Vehicles	776	1,716
Number of Query Images	1678	-

Table 2. MatchRate of our Model

Methods	Match Rate	Front	Back	Left	Right
ResNet [25]		79.52	79.82	77.01	76.90
Inception V-3 [24]	Rank-1	81.56	80.95	79.89	79.10
Our Model		84.92	84.05	83.73	82.60
ResNet [25]		81.16	81.01	80.75	78.99
Inception V-3 [24]	Rank-5	83.45	82.99	81.44	80.81
Our Model		87.89	86.88	86.63	85.11

4.2 Experimental Settings

Evaluation method description is as follow. In this paper, we have used query set 1678 images in the VeRi dataset for evaluation. The network is trained on NVIDIA Titan X GPU. We used Cumulative Match Characteristic CMC curve for evaluation metric reflecting the correct matching rate. The experiments performed a few times to ensure stability. **Experimental environment** includes Ubuntu 16.04.5 LTS OS, GPU NVIDIA TITAN X.

4.3 Network Training

We trained these two Inception V-3 [24] and ResNet [25] on our network, we trained our network on CompCars [10] and VeRi [9] and tested it on VeRi dataset then it generates probability maps associated to different sides, probability maps are used as weights. Our model shows that it is capable of decently localizing pose variation and occlusion.

Evaluation Metrics. To evaluate the performance of the method, we used CMC and mAP, which are standard for re-id problems, however, CMC represents the percentage that the correct match is included in the best match.

Table 3. RANK-1, RANK-5 and map accuracies of the comparison methods on veri dataset [9]

Methods	Match rate	Front	Back	Left	Right
VGG+Triplet Loss [26]		40.40	35.40	31.90	30.17
VGG+CCL [3]	Rank-1	43.60	37.00	32.90	31.10
Mixed Diff + CLL [3]		49.00	42.80	38.20	37.60
Our Model		84.92	84.05	83.73	82.60
VGG+Triplet Loss [26]		61.70	54.60	50.30	50.10
VGG+CCL [3]	Rank-5	64.20	57.10	53.30	50.88
Mixed Diff + CLL [3]		73.50	66.80	61.60	60.89
Our Model		87.89	86.88	86.63	85.11
Our Model	mAP	71.64	69.88	69.54	68.11

- **Cumulative matching curve(CMC):** it is used as a measurement for performance of identification system measured as 1:m.
- **Mean Average Precision (mAP):** Precision is the ratio of true positives (TP) and the sum of true positives and false positives (FP).

$$Precision = \frac{TP}{TP + FP} \tag{1}$$

Average Precision combines recall and precision for retrieval of ranked results. It is mean of precision scores after retrieval of each relevant image.

$$AP = \sum_{l=1}^{n} \frac{p(l)g(l)}{G_t} \tag{2}$$

where n is the total number of test images and G_t is the number of ground truth images. However, p*(l)* is precision at lth position, and g*(l)* is the function at value of l as a indicator and if the match is found at lth or not. The arithmetic mean of average precision for a set of Q query images is called mean average precision (mAP) and is formulated as.

$$mAP = \sum_{k=1}^{Q} \frac{AP(k)}{Q} \tag{3}$$

- **Rank:** It measures the similarity of a test image with its class image. For example. If t1 which is test1 image corresponds to class1 and it is found in top1 then it is said to be rank@1, however, if it is found in top 5 then it's called rank@5 and so on.

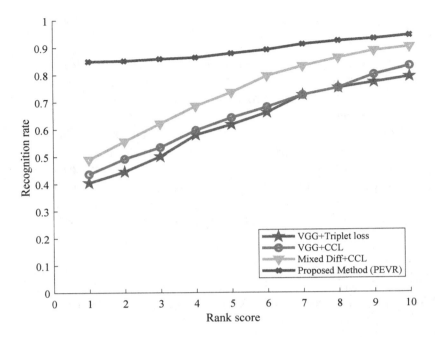

Fig. 3. CMC Curve on Proposed method along with other state-of-art methods.

4.4 Comparison with Baseline Methods

We use ResNet as a baseline method. The comparison results are shown in Table 2. It is shown in the table that features extracted by inception-V3 obtains better performance than ResNet. Each network can learn feature from training, but the learning ability varies for every network while taking weighted sum led us to categories the sides with better performance.

4.5 Comparison with State-of-art Methods

To evaluate the effectiveness of our method, we tested and provided the results in Table 3. We have compared our approach with different state-of-art methods including VGG+CCL [3], VGG+Triplet Loss [26] and Mixed Diff + CLL [3] and achieved better performance, the results can be seen in Table 3.

We can see our method achieved significantly more accuracy in Rank-1 than other state-of-art methods, and even better in Rank-5. PEVR can minimize intra-class differences and maximizes the inter-class difference at the same time and is fit for the task. We repeated the testing phase to evaluate the model prediction accuracy and got the CMC curve as shown in Fig. 3. Match rate from rank-1 to rank-5 of the proposed method. We used the manually split dataset to train our network, Table 3 shows the rank-1 and rank-5 along with mAP of our method compared with the other three methods. From results, its a significant margin of increment of 20% to 30% compared with previous methods our PEVR performed better.

5   Conclusion

In this paper, we propose a pose estimation method for vehicle Re-Id (PEVR) model for estimating pose. Our method is less computationally expensive and achieved significant results compare with other methods. Driving direction can be found by estimating the pose of vehicle in future work. Our method also collaborates with visual features, we demonstrate that indeed a simple network, if trained properly on a large number of image dataset can outperform other methods. The results show a significant improvement in efficiency and accuracy.

References

1. Zhang, Y., Bai, Y., Ding, M., Li, Y., Ghanem, B.: W2f: a weakly-supervised to fully-supervised framework for object detection. In: The IEEE Conference on Computer Vision and Pattern Recognition (CVPR), June 2018
2. Mahendran, S., Vidal, R.: Car segmentation and pose estimation using 3d object models (2015)
3. Liu, H., Tian, Y., Yang, Y., Pang, L., Huang, T.: Deep relative distance learning: tell the difference between similar vehicles. In: The IEEE Conference on Computer Vision and Pattern Recognition (CVPR), June 2016
4. Ahmed, M.J., Sarfraz, M., Zidouri, A., Al-Khatib, W.G.: License plate recognition system. In: 10th IEEE International Conference on Electronics, Circuits and Systems, 2003. ICECS 2003. Proceedings of the 2003, vol. 2, pp. 898–901 (2003)
5. Bulan, O., Kozitsky, V., Ramesh, P., Shreve, M.: Segmentation- and annotation-free license plate recognition with deep localization and failure identification. IEEE Trans. Intell. Transp. Syst. 18(9), 2351–2363 (2017)
6. Anagnostopoulos, C.N.E., Anagnostopoulos, I.E., Loumos, V., Kayafas, E.: A license plate-recognition algorithm for intelligent transportation system applications. IEEE Trans. Intell. Transp. Syst. 7(3), 377–392 (2006)
7. Ahmed, E., Jones, M., Marks, T.K.: An improved deep learning architecture for person re-identification. In: The IEEE Conference on Computer Vision and Pattern Recognition (CVPR), June 2015
8. Xiao, T., Li, H., Ouyang, W., Wang, X.: Learning deep feature representations with domain guided dropout for person re-identification. In: The IEEE Conference on Computer Vision and Pattern Recognition (CVPR), June 2016
9. Liu, X., Liu, W., Ma, H., Fu, H.: Large-scale vehicle re-identification in urban surveillance videos. In: 2016 IEEE International Conference on Multimedia and Expo (ICME), pp. 1–6, July 2016
10. Yang, L., Luo, P., Loy, C.C., Tang, X.: A large-scale car dataset for fine-grained categorization and verification. In: 2015 IEEE Conference on Computer Vision and Pattern Recognition (CVPR), pp. 3973–3981, June 2015
11. Sun, Y., Wang, X., Tang, X.: Deep learning face representation from predicting 10,000 classes. In: The IEEE Conference on Computer Vision and Pattern Recognition (CVPR), June 2014

12. Sun, Y., Chen, Y., Wang, X., Tang, X.: Deep learning face representation by joint identification-verification. In: Ghahramani, Z., Welling, M., Cortes, C., Lawrence, N.D., Weinberger, K.Q. (eds.) Advances in Neural Information Processing Systems 27, pp. 1988–1996. Curran Associates, Inc. (2014)
13. Sun, Y., Liang, D., Wang, X., Tang, X.: Deepid3: Face recognition with very deep neural networks (2015)
14. Wen, Y., Zhang, K., Li, Z., Qiao, Y.: A discriminative feature learning approach for deep face recognition. In: Leibe, B., Matas, J., Sebe, N., Welling, M. (eds.) ECCV 2016. LNCS, vol. 9911, pp. 499–515. Springer, Cham (2016). https://doi.org/10.1007/978-3-319-46478-7_31
15. Taigman, Y., Yang, M., Ranzato, M., Wolf, L.: Deepface: Closing the gap to human-level performance in face verification. In: The IEEE Conference on Computer Vision and Pattern Recognition (CVPR), June 2014
16. Liao, S., Hu, Y., Zhu, X., Li, S.Z.: Person re-identification by local maximal occurrence representation and metric learning. In: The IEEE Conference on Computer Vision and Pattern Recognition (CVPR), June 2015
17. Liao, S., Hu, Y., Li, S.Z.: Joint dimension reduction and metric learning for person re-identification. arXiv preprint arXiv:1406.4216 (2014)
18. Feris, R.S., et al.: Large-scale vehicle detection, indexing, and search in urban surveillance videos. IEEE Trans. Multimedia **14**(1), 28–42 (2012)
19. Matei, B.C., Sawhney, H.S., Samarasekera, S.: Vehicle tracking across nonoverlapping cameras using joint kinematic and appearance features. CVPR **2011**, 3465–3472 (2011)
20. Liu, X., Zhang, S., Huang, Q., Gao, W.: Ram: a region-aware deep model for vehicle re-identification. In: 2018 IEEE International Conference on Multimedia and Expo (ICME), pp. 1–6, July 2018
21. Liu, X., Liu, W., Mei, T., Ma, H.: Provid: progressive and multimodal vehicle reidentification for large-scale urban surveillance. IEEE Trans. Multimedia **20**(3), 645–658 (2018)
22. Khare, V., et al.: A novel character segmentation-reconstruction approach for license plate recognition. Expert Syst. Appl. **131**, 219–239 (2019)
23. Hendry, Chen, R.C.: Automatic license plate recognition via sliding-window darknet-yolo deep learning. Image Vis. Comput. **87**, 47–56 (2019)
24. Szegedy, C., Vanhoucke, V., Ioffe, S., Shlens, J., Wojna, Z.: Rethinking the inception architecture for computer vision. In: The IEEE Conference on Computer Vision and Pattern Recognition (CVPR), June 2016
25. He, K., Zhang, X., Ren, S., Sun, J.: Deep residual learning for image recognition. In: The IEEE Conference on Computer Vision and Pattern Recognition (CVPR), June 2016
26. Ding, S., Lin, L., Wang, G., Chao, H.: Deep feature learning with relative distance comparison for person re-identification. Pattern Recogn. **48**(10), 2993–3003 (2015)

The Research of Chinese Ethnical Face Recognition Based on Deep Learning

Qike Zhao[1,2(✉)], Tangming Chen[2], Xiaosu Zhu[2], and Jingkuan Song[1,2]

[1] Guizhou Provincial Key Laboratory of Public Big Data, GuiZhou University,
Guiyang 550025, Guizhou, China
kebounden@gmail.com, jingkuan.song@gmail.com
[2] Center for Future Media, University of Electronic Science and Technology of China,
Chengdu, China
tangmingchen8@gmail.com, xiaosu.zhu@outlook.com

Abstract. Face recognition emerged in the seventies. With the introduction of deep learning methods, especially the convolution neural networks (CNNs), more and more traditional machine learning techniques have been recently superseded by them. In a multi-ethnic country like China, the study for Chinese ethnical face recognition (CEFR) has practical demands and applications. In this paper, we provide a brief of popular face recognition procedure based on deep learning method firstly. Then, as lacking of the corresponding dataset, we construct a collection of Chinese ethnical face images (CCEFI) including Han, Uygur, Tibetan and Mongolian. Based on multi-task cascaded convolution networks (MTCNN) [14] and residual networks (ResNets) [11,12], our proposed model can achieve promising results for face detection and classification. Specifically, the average precision reaches 75% on CCEFI self-draft. Experimental results indicate that our model is able to detect the face in some constrained environments and distinguish its ethnical category. Meanwhile, the dataset established by us would be a useful dataset for relevant work.

Keywords: Chinese ethnical face recognition · Convolutional neural network · Residual network · Face detection

1 Introduction

Face recognition refers to the technology capable of identifying or verifying the identity of subjects in images or videos. The first face recognition algorithm was developed in the early seventies [13]. Since then, related work have continued and the accuracy has been also improved gradually. Nowadays face recognition has been widely applied and accepted in various occasions, such as access control, fraud detection, monitoring system and social media. One pivotal factor is its non-intrusive nature [28]. For example, in modern face recognition system the user just needs to stand in the field of view of a camera to finish an authentication.

© Springer Nature Switzerland AG 2019
J. Song and X. Zhu (Eds.): APWeb-WAIM 2019 Workshops, LNCS 11809, pp. 79–91, 2019.
https://doi.org/10.1007/978-3-030-33982-1_7

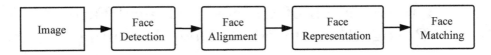

Fig. 1. Face recognition building blocks.

The technique has shifted significantly over the year accompanied with the rise of some excellent deep learning algorithms [20, 22–25] and large-scale datasets. Traditional methods rely on hand-crafted features, such as edges and texture description, combined with machine learning techniques, such as principal component analysis (PCA), linear discriminant analysis (LDA) or support vector machines(SVM). The hand-crafted features, lacking of robustness in most cases, are far from the industrial demands encountered in unconstrained environments. In contrast, Deep learning method based on CNNs could be trained with large datasets to learn the best features to represent the clusters of data. Recently, there are a mass of available collections of face in-the-wild on the web [2, 17, 18, 24]. CNN-based face recognition trained in these resources have achieved higher accuracy, accounting for they learn the features that are robust to the real-world variations. They out-perform than traditional ones in practice.

Face recognition systems are usually composed of the following blocks, as shown in Fig. 1:

(1) **Face Detection.** The face detection finds the face objects in the image, then returns the coordinates of bounding box that mark the position of target objects. This is illustrated in Fig. 2(a).
(2) **Face Alignment.** The purpose of face alignment is to scale and crop face images, at the same time to find a set of reference points, such as left and right eyes, nose and mouse's left and right etc. as shown in Fig. 2(b). They are also called facials landmarks.
(3) **Face Representation.** During the face representation stage, the pixel values of image are transformed into the compact vector that represent the features of the face.
(4) **Face Matching.** In this block, vectors or templates are compared to each others, and ultimately the model would count a score that indicates the similarity of them.

The growth in popularity of deep learning methods has been dynamic. More and more researchers apply the approaches to many other computer vision tasks, even combine with the fields of humanity and sociology [5, 8]. In this paper we also make full use of the prevalent methods to solve the CEFR-task. In short, the CEFR-task is a classification problem to judge which Chinese minority group they belong to in the pictures or videos, by analyzing the ethnical characteristics of face.

The ethnical characteristics are important parts of facial features. In the investigation of minority groups in China, the facial features are usually summarized into series of text description, in the forms of survey and measurement

Fig. 2. The images contain two procedures of face recognition. In (a), face detection designates the bounding boxes for faces. In (b), the faces are cropped, and reference points are drawn.

on the counterparts. For example, the research group [31] describes the facial features of Tibetans: The hair is dark and straight, the eyes' color is mostly brown, the rate of internal pleats is higher, the extraocular angle is higher than the internal, the degree of eye cracking is moderately narrow, the bridge of nose is straight, the lip is slightly convex, the humerus is prominent and the face is wide and flat. This also proves that the national characteristics are extractable and quantifiable, and indicates a direction to design the algorithm on extracting ethnical face features.

It is required to establish an ear classification criterion. Researchers generally use racial categories as identification labels [1,4]. The broadest ethnic category criteria are: Africans and African-Americans, Caucasians, East Asians, Native Americans, Pacific Islanders, Indians, and Latinos. The sum of all these categories are able to cover approximately 95% of the world's population. In some cases, a part of nations can be identified by naked eyes, which leads to an illusion: it is easy to understand and realize the ethnical face recognition, but in fact, the underlying algorithm is complex and diverse.

Above all, there is no unified interpretation of the definition of the nation, and the definition of ambiguity causes uncertainty. Secondly, with the continuous development of modern society, nation migration and integration have become the mainstream, which will inevitably lead to new changes in national characteristics, even blurring. On the other hand, due to the influence of social factors, such as prejudice and inherent thinking on some nations, the task is up against some practical troubles both in data collection and experimentation. In current, the research on CEFR is very rare, and there is no public standard dataset.

2   Proposed Approach

In this section, we will describe our approach towards setting up a reliable as well as available ethnical face dataset, and joint face detection and recognition.

2.1   Collection of Chinese Ethnical Face Image

CCEFI Dataset. CCEFI is the one containing four different ethnical groups set by us. As for a face recognition system, a good training set directly affects the accuracy of system identification. And a high-quality training set means enough and well-crafted samples. Datasets similar to application scenarios often perform well in practice and own better generalization capabilities.

At present, amounts of face datasets are available on web [2, 17, 18, 24], at the meantime the related recognition competitions [10] tend to be more intricacy and mature. In China, there is also CAS-PEAL collected by [9], including the variable factors like pose, expression, accessory and lighting, but the samples are mostly the Han nationality. We refer to the same way [19] using web crawler to set up CCEFI dataset. In order to establish a high quality collection, the work [15] gathers the minority students in campus to collect face images. It is also a feasible method.

In initial search process, it is necessary to clarify the requirements of CCEFI dataset self-built including the following points:

(1) Select ethnic groups with obvious facial features: Mongolian, Tibetan, Uygur, and Han nationality, mainly for Han and Uygur.
(2) Only the frontal face images under unconstrained conditions are accepted. Meanwhile, the images are required to be certain clarity, and it allows a little noise influences, such as makeup and illumination, etc.
(3) Ethnical images are required to be preprocessed by face detection and segmentation module. The processed serve as the input of classification block.
(4) According to experimental results on classification, further screening photographs is essential, which insures the quality of dataset and correctness of labels.

Web Crawler. Based the definition by Wikipedia, web crawler [29] is an internet bot that systematically browses the worldwide web, typically for the purpose of web indexing. It is a momentous method to gather datasets in many works. Our implementation of the web crawler is based on the open source crawler framework, WebMagic on Github, which is written in Java and possesses good extensibility. By means of rewriting functions according to different requirements, users could achieve crawling steadily and efficiently.

The main process includes following blocks:

(1) **Download.** The block integrates the interfaces of page download and preprocess. In the process of crawling web pages, http requests are required, and WebMagic encapsulates Apache HttpClient as a download tool by

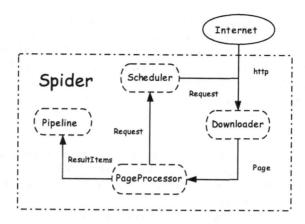

Fig. 3. Main blocks of WebMagic.

default, with powerful redirection, connection multiplexing, and proxy settings (Fig. 3).

(2) **PageProcessor.** The block implements parsing pages in target line and is able to extract the candidate links in current page.

(3) **Schedule.** The block is responsible for managing the URL to be crawled. The scheduler module can be shared by multiple spiders for versatility.

(4) **Pipeline.** It reprocesses the content acquired by PageProcessor, including disposing data and storing results into files or databases.

(5) **Spider.** This module is an entry of the program. By means of filling the parameters, it is easy to achieve creating, starting, stopping and multi-threading of the crawler.

We take the process of crawling Tibetan images as an example. We crawl the introduction pictures and album covers of singer on the website http://www. 25xz.com/index.shtml. Similar operation is executed on the news site http:// www.tibet.cn. At the meantime, it is feasible to collect images via Bing Image Search. During image collection, there exit many engineering problems that mainly include programs adapting to dynamic pages and being against to anti-reptile mechanism. The crawling processes for Mongolian, Uygur, and Han are alike.

2.2 Face Detection

Some available face detection and face alignment method ignore the inherent correlation between these two tasks. Now several works attempting to jointly solve them [3,30] are proposed. We refer the work [14] that presents a novel framework to integrate these two tasks using unified cascaded CNNs by multi-task learning with high detection accuracy and fast running speed.

The CNNs architecture consists of three stages. Firstly, it produces candidate windows also called bounding boxes through a shallow CNNs. Then, it refines the windows through another complex CNNs. Finally, it uses the more powerful one to select the top one result containing bounding box and facial landmarks positions. And it leverages three tasks to train the detectors: face/non-face classification, bounding box regression, and facial landmarks localization.

In first task, the learning objective is formulated as a binary classification problem. For each sample x_i, we use the cross-entropy loss:

$$L_i^{det} = -(y_i^{det} \log(p_i) + (1 - y_i^{det})(1 - \log(p_i))) \tag{1}$$

where p_i is the probability produced by the network that indicates a sample being a face. The notation $y_i^{det} \in \{0, 1\}$ denotes the ground-truth label.

For each candidate window, we compute the offset between it and nearest ground truth (i.e., the bounding boxes' left top, height and width). The learning objective is formulated as a regression problem. Hence, we employ the Euclidean loss for each sample x_i:

$$L_i^{box} = \|y_i^{\hat{box}} - y_i^{box}\|_2^2 \tag{2}$$

where $y_i^{\hat{box}}$ is the regression result obtained from the network and y_i^{box} is the ground-truth coordinate, including left top, height and width, and thus $y_i^{box} \in \mathbb{R}^4$.

Similar to the former, facial landmark detection is also formulated as a regression problem:

$$L_i^{landmark} = \|y_i^{landma\hat{r}k} - y_i^{landmark}\|_2^2 \tag{3}$$

where $y_i^{landma\hat{r}k}$ is the facial landmark's target coordinates, and $y_i^{landmark}$ is the ground-truth coordinates. There are five facial landmarks, including left eye, right eye, nose, left mouse corner, and right mouse corner, and thus $y_i^{landmark} \in \mathbb{R}^{10}$.

The overall learning target can be formulated as:

$$\min \sum_{i=1}^{N} \sum_{j \in det, box, landmark} \alpha_j \beta_i^j L_i^j \tag{4}$$

where N is the number of training samples. α_j denotes on the task importance and each stage owns different value. β_j^i is sample type indicator. For example, the non-face image in training process only has task of bounding box regression, therefore the loss functions expressed in Eqs. (3), (4) are not used. In this case, it is natural to employ stochastic gradient descent to train the CNNs.

2.3   Face Recognition

After scaling and cropping the face images, it is required to classify the ethnic groups by deep learning methods.

Recently, residual networks (ResNets) [11] has become the preferred choice for many objects recognition tasks, including face recognition [7,16]. The main idea of ResNets is the introduction of building block that uses shortcut connection to learn a residual mapping, as shown in Fig. 4. The use of shortcut connection

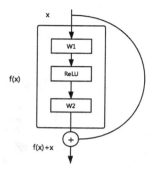

Fig. 4. Original residual block proposed in [11].

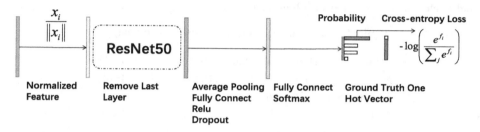

Fig. 5. We train a ResNet architecture with common fine-tuning methods, to achieve face classification of ethnical groups. By the way, the paper [11] proposes five basic residual networks models, and in this task we choose ResNet50.

allows the training of much deeper architectures more easier than "plain" ones. The reason is that the former network facilitates the flow of information across layers effectively than the latter, and converges more quickly, which has been widely proved experimentally.

We use ResNets to extract the feature map in face images, then fine-tune the structure in common manners. It could use classification loss function, cross-entropy loss, presented as follows:

$$L_i^{class} = -\log \frac{e^{p_i}}{\sum_{j=1}^{n} e^{p_j}} \tag{5}$$

where p_i denotes the probability of i-th sample belonging to the y_i-th class. The number of classes is n, and corresponding network structure is shown in Fig. 5.

3   Experiments

In this section, we firstly show the information of CCEFI self-draft, the face images of which have been preprocessed by detection and cropping module. The images are directly the input objects of the classification networks. Then we

(a) Single-face target.   (b) Mutlti-face target.

Fig. 6. The face detector based on MTCNN correctly finds the faces in different pictures and circles the face objects with bounding box.

Table 1. The number of various ethnical face images.

Ethnicity	Han	Mongolian	Tibetan	Uygur	Total
Number	1058	620	1732	904	4314
Training Set	846	496	1388	722	3452
Test Set	212	124	344	182	862

compare the diverse structures: ResNet50, VGG19 [21], Inception-V3 [27], and Inception-ResNet-V2 [26]. All of them, with models pre-trained in ImageNet [6], are based on the deep learning framework of Keras.

3.1 Preparation

As shown in Fig. 6, the faces in the ethnic images are effectively detected, whether it is a single-face target or a multi-face target. And we also display the face images cropped in Fig. 7.

After filtration and statistics, the numbers of face images of each ethnic group are stated in Table 1, and the training and test set are divided randomly as the proportion around 4:1.

3.2 Results

Under the condition of multiple experiments, the accuracies of training set on ResNet50, Inception-V3, and Inception-ResNet-V2 after 40 epoches round reach 98%. For the test sets, the values stay around 70%–75%. The CNNs reformed from VGG19 scores the accuracy of 60%–65% both in training and test set.

For the purpose to explain the results in more detail, we present the confusion matrixes of the four networks, shown in Table 2, and the following viewpoints are summarized.

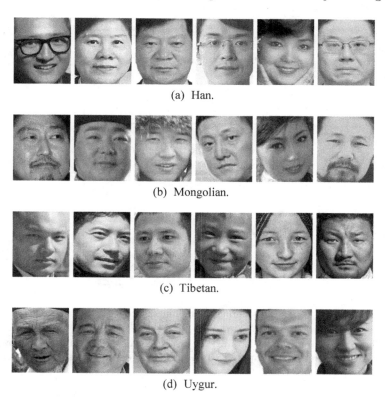

(a) Han.

(b) Mongolian.

(c) Tibetan.

(d) Uygur.

Fig. 7. The images contain the people with appropriate face angles but different ages and genders, and these samples mostly avoid the clear covers on face after filtrating by us. Except the common, there are also some singers and actors with popular makeup, which consequently increases the difficulty for the discriminator.

Except for VGG19, the test accuracies of the other three networks are similar, but the training time of the ResNet50 is faster. The Inception-ResNet-V2 model introduces the idea of residual networks, which enables the networks to develop into a deeper level and be easy to train. At the same time, it introduces the idea of Inception blocks to optimize the structure of each layer by widening the singer-layer network. It increases the adaptability to the scale. Correspondingly, the network costs more and the training duration is the longest, and the classification effect should be optimal. However, after many experiments, we found that accuracy of 75% is the bottleneck in the test set. It may be related to the quantity and quality of the dataset. Same situation occurs in the paper [19].

Among the four sets of results, Mongolian is easier identified as Tibetan, but Tibetan is not easily identified as Mongolian. In VGG19, even most of Mongolian are considered to be Tibetan. After analyzing the training and test set, we find:

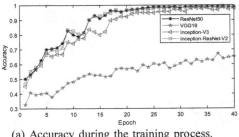

(a) Accuracy during the training process.

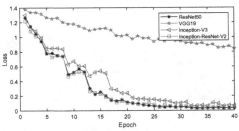

(b) Loss during the training process.

Fig. 8. The other three networks start to converge after 20 rounds. It shows that VGG19 is difficult to train compared to the other three networks under the current dataset.

(1) In terms of quantity, since the collection of Mongolian is the smallest of all sets, only containing 620 pictures, the result is likely fluctuating.
(2) With regard of access approach, both Mongolian and Tibetan are acquired from singers, while the other two groups do not have such approach. The ethnical singers could not represent the ordinary well because of their makeup. Furthermore, singers have coincidences, so it is easy to confuse. There are more ways to attain the images for Tibetan than Mongolian, which results in the recognition of Tibetan owning robustness than the others.
(3) This problem also indicates a certain over-fitting phenomenon.

Finally on the binary classification of Han and Uygur, the recognition accuracy reaches 90%, which states a certain application space (Fig. 8).

Table 2. Confusion matrixes of results on four architectures

ResNet50	Training time of each epoch: **35 s**			
	Test accuracy: **74.06%**			
	Han	Mongolian	Tibetan	Uygur
Han	**74.06%**	4.25%	11.32%	10.38%
Mongolian	10.48%	**45.97%**	31.45%	12.10%
Tibetan	8.43%	4.65%	**79.94%**	6.98%
Uygur	7.14%	2.75%	6.04%	**84.07%**
VGG19	Training time of each epoch: **25 s**			
	Test accuracy: **62.50**			
	Han	Mongolian	Tibetan	Uygur
Han	**64.15%**	0.47%	22.17%	13.21%
Mongolian	7.26%	**10.48%**	68.55%	13.71%
Tibetan	9.88%	5.52%	**72.38%**	12.21%
Uygur	9.89%	4.40%	21.43%	**64.29%**
Inception-V3	Training time of each epoch: **41 s**			
	Test accuracy: **71.25%**			
	Han	Mongolian	Tibetan	Uygur
Han	**78.30%**	3.30%	10.38%	8.02%
Mongolian	13.71%	**55.65%**	25.00%	5.65%
Tibetan	9.59%	14.53%	**71.80%**	4.07%
Uygur	9.89%	3.30%	6.04%	**80.77%**
Inception-ResNet-V2	Training time of each epoch: **92 s**			
	Test accuracy: **72.81%**			
	Han	Mongolian	Tibetan	Uygur
Han	**73.11%**	4.72%	14.15%	8.02%
Mongolian	10.48%	**57.26%**	25.00%	7.26%
Tibetan	7.27%	12.21%	**77.33%**	3.20%
Uygur	6.04%	3.85%	4.95%	**85.16%**

4 Conclusion

This paper starts from the current situation and prospect of face recognition, and introduces the our task both in practical significance and implementation direction.

Lacking of open ethnical face dataset, we build a collection of Chinese ethnical face images (CCEFI) dataset including Han, Uygur, Tibetan and Mongolian through web crawlers. The CCEFI self-draft includes multiple variations, e.g. different genders and ages, makeup and illumination, etc. in non-restrictive occasions with large differences. The total picture number of CCEFI reaches nearly 4500. Then we design MTCNN-based face detection module and ResNet-based face classification module. Experimental results demonstrate that the model can detect the faces in photos, then classify the ethnical groups they belong to. In the future, we will ameliorate the quality and quantity of CCEFI, and supplement other ethnical groups.

Acknowledgements. This work is supported by Major Scientific and Technological Special Project of Guizhou Province (20183002).

References

1. Barbujani, G.: Human races: classifying people vs understanding diversity. Curr. Genomics **6**(4), 215–226 (2005)
2. Cao, Q., Shen, L., Xie, W., Parkhi, O.M., Zisserman, A.: VGGFace2: a dataset for recognising faces across pose and age. In: 2018 13th IEEE International Conference on Automatic Face & Gesture Recognition (FG 2018), pp. 67–74. IEEE (2018)
3. Chen, D., Ren, S., Wei, Y., Cao, X., Sun, J.: Joint cascade face detection and alignment. In: Fleet, D., Pajdla, T., Schiele, B., Tuytelaars, T. (eds.) ECCV 2014. LNCS, vol. 8694, pp. 109–122. Springer, Cham (2014). https://doi.org/10.1007/978-3-319-10599-4_8
4. Coon, C.S.: The origin of races (1962)
5. Delorme, A., Pierce, A., Michel, L., Radin, D.: Prediction of mortality based on facial characteristics. Front. Hum. Neurosci. **10**, 173 (2016). https://doi.org/10.3389/fnhum.2016.00173
6. Deng, J., Dong, W., Socher, R., Li, L.J., Li, K., Fei-Fei, L.: ImageNet: a large-scale hierarchical image database. In: 2009 IEEE Conference on Computer Vision and Pattern Recognition, pp. 248–255. IEEE (2009)
7. Deng, J., Guo, J., Xue, N., Zafeiriou, S.: ArcFace: additive angular margin loss for deep face recognition. arXiv preprint arXiv:1801.07698 (2018)
8. Fu, S., He, H., Hou, Z.: Learning race from face: a survey. IEEE Trans. Pattern Anal. Mach. Intell. **36**(12), 2483–2509 (2014). https://doi.org/10.1109/TPAMI.2014.2321570
9. Gao, W., et al.: The cas-peal large-scale chinese face database and baseline evaluations. IEEE Trans. Syst. Man Cybern. Part A Syst. Hum. **38**(1), 149–161 (2007)
10. Grother, P., Ngan, M.: Face recognition vendor test (FRVT). NIST interagency report (8009) (2018)
11. He, K., Zhang, X., Ren, S., Sun, J.: Deep residual learning for image recognition. In: Computer Vision and Pattern Recognition, pp. 770–778 (2016)
12. He, K., Zhang, X., Ren, S., Sun, J.: Identity mappings in deep residual networks. In: Leibe, B., Matas, J., Sebe, N., Welling, M. (eds.) ECCV 2016. LNCS, vol. 9908, pp. 630–645. Springer, Cham (2016). https://doi.org/10.1007/978-3-319-46493-0_38
13. Kelly, M.D.: Visual identification of people by computer. Technical report, Stanford Univ Calif Dept of Computer Science (1970)
14. Li, H., Lin, Z., Shen, X., Brandt, J., Hua, G.: A convolutional neural network cascade for face detection, pp. 5325–5334 (2015)
15. Liu, H.: Research on facial recognition of china ethnic minorities. MS thesis, Northeastern University (2009)
16. Liu, W., Wen, Y., Yu, Z., Meng, Y.: Large-margin softmax loss for convolutional neural networks. In: International Conference on International Conference on Machine Learning (2016)

17. Nech, A., Kemelmacher-Shlizerman, I.: Level playing field for million scale face recognition. In: Proceedings of the IEEE Conference on Computer Vision and Pattern Recognition, pp. 7044–7053 (2017)
18. Parkhi, O.M., Vedaldi, A., Zisserman, A., et al.: Deep face recognition. In: BMVC, vol. 1, p. 6 (2015)
19. Qiu, S.: The research of face ethnicity recognition base on deep learning. MS thesis, South China University of Technology (2016)
20. Schroff, F., Kalenichenko, D., Philbin, J.: FaceNet: a unified embedding for face recognition and clustering-1a_089. pdf (2015)
21. Simonyan, K., Zisserman, A.: Very deep convolutional networks for large-scale image recognition. arXiv preprint arXiv:1409.1556 (2014)
22. Sun, Y., Chen, Y., Wang, X., Tang, X.: Deep learning face representation by joint identification-verification. In: Advances in Neural Information Processing Systems, pp. 1988–1996 (2014)
23. Sun, Y., Liang, D., Wang, X., Tang, X.: DeepID3: face recognition with very deep neural networks. arXiv preprint arXiv:1502.00873 (2015)
24. Sun, Y., Wang, X., Tang, X.: Deep learning face representation from predicting 10,000 classes, pp. 1891–1898 (2014)
25. Sun, Y., Wang, X., Tang, X.: Deeply learned face representations are sparse, selective, and robust. In: Proceedings of the IEEE Conference on Computer Vision and Pattern Recognition, pp. 2892–2900 (2015)
26. Szegedy, C., Ioffe, S., Vanhoucke, V., Alemi, A.A.: Inception-v4, inception-resnet and the impact of residual connections on learning. In: Thirty-First AAAI Conference on Artificial Intelligence (2017)
27. Szegedy, C., Vanhoucke, V., Ioffe, S., Shlens, J., Wojna, Z.: Rethinking the inception architecture for computer vision. In: Proceedings of the IEEE Conference on Computer Vision and Pattern Recognition, pp. 2818–2826 (2016)
28. Trigueros, D.S., Meng, L., Hartnett, M.: Face recognition: from traditional to deep learning methods. arXiv preprint arXiv:1811.00116 (2018)
29. Wikipedia Contributors: Web crawler – Wikipedia, the free encyclopedia (2019). https://en.wikipedia.org/w/index.php?title=Web_crawler&oldid=900366065. Accessed 11 June 2019
30. Zhang, C., Zhang, Z.: Improving multiview face detection with multi-task deep convolutional neural networks. In: IEEE Winter Conference on Applications of Computer Vision, pp. 1036–1041. IEEE (2014)
31. Zhang, Z.: Institutional characteristics of the tibetan people. Acta Anthropologica Sinica **12**, 250–257 (1985)

Model of Charging Stations Construction and Electric Vehicles Development Prediction

Qilong Zhang[1,2](✉), Zheyong Qiu[3], and Jingkuan Song[1,2]

[1] Guizhou Provincial Key Laboratory of Public Big Data,
GuiZhou University, Guiyang 550025, Guizhou, China
qilong.zhangdl@gmail.com
[2] Center for Future Media, University of Electronic Science
and Technology of China, Chengdu, China
[3] Hangzhou Dianzi University, Hangzhou, China

Abstract. Electric vehicle is attracting more and more people and the construction of charging stations is becoming very important. Our paper mainly deals with the construction of charging stations and electric vehicles market penetration. First, through the relationship between charging stations and gas stations quantitatively in America, we evaluate 501,474 charging stations will be built in 2060, among which there is 334,316 supercharging stations and 167,158 destination-charging stations. Second, we study the optimal distribution of charging stations in South Korea, and establish a bi-objective programming based on Cooperative Covering model with the help of Queue Theory. Combining these two models we find the optimal number of charging stations is 30,045. Thirdly, we use logistic growth model to estimate the growth of charging stations. We predict that South Korea will achieve 10% electric vehicles in 2030, 30% in 2036, and 50% in 2040. Combining factors of charging stations, national policies and international initiatives, etc. we infer South Korea will realize all electric vehicles in at latest 2060. Lastly, we utilize K-means to classify those countries into three classes.

Keywords: Cooperative Covering Model · Logistic Growth · Queuing Theory · K-means

1 Introduction

In recent decades, with the increasing pressure of environment and economy, people are more and more interested in electric vehicles. A variety of factors need to be considered comprehensively for the mathematical model of electric charging station construction. Due to the lack of data, we can only acquire 5 years' specific number of vehicles. But we can search relevant data about American gas station, gas price, etc. When vehicles are transferred to all-electric ones, gas station will be replaced by charging station as they play similar roles in daily life.

© Springer Nature Switzerland AG 2019
J. Song and X. Zhu (Eds.): APWeb-WAIM 2019 Workshops, LNCS 11809, pp. 92–104, 2019.
https://doi.org/10.1007/978-3-030-33982-1_8

So, it's easy to associate these two kinds of stations. Thus, we adopt the idea of On Comparison to derive the number of charging stations from gas stations. For the coverage model, there are roughly three options through the study of scholars: maximum coverage model [2,4], cooperative coverage model [3,5], and gradual coverage model [16]. We combine the advantages of these three models and adopt a decentralized cooperative gradual coverage model. The queuing theory [8] can better simulate the arrival of customers and facilitate the construction of charging stations. In addition, the Logistic growth model in biology can also be used to scientifically predict the future development of electric vehicles.

2   Related Work

On Comparison. A common used method in setting labor quota, is based on producing or completing the quota of the same type of product or process, to derive that of the other kind of product or process through comparison and analysis. The two products to be compared must be similar or of the same type, in the same series, and are clearly comparable. For our problem, gas station and charging station have close effects on human life and comparable operation mode. Therefore, the number and distribution of charging station may have similar rules with gas station.

Coverage Model. Different covering models have different focuses. Li et al believed that the supporting equipment of the charging station was small and did not need to occupy additional land. However, due to the long charging time, it was most suitable for charging in the user-oriented parking process, and it was suitable for adopting a decentralized coverage layout, so the maximum coverage model was adopted [18]. However, it is not comprehensive to only consider the number of charging stations, because for the radiation radius of charging stations, the closer the distance is, the more advantageous the area should be. So Nie Li chose to use the method of gradual coverage site selection [16]. In addition, with the increasing popularity of electric vehicles, it is not feasible to only consider the centralized construction of charging stations in a few addresses. Just as what Li et al said, it is necessary to build charging stations separately, so as to give owners more choices. Therefore, [2–5] adopted the cooperative coverage model.

Queue Model. When considering the design of charging stations, it must be noted that even if quick charging piles are used, it will take 30 min to be fully charged, which is different from ordinary car refueling and the speed is much slower than this. Therefore, it is also an important factor for the queuing model [8], By adopting the queuing theory model, Zhou Yong et al. can better simulate the arrival state of vehicles and the time of waiting, so that we can weigh the waiting time and the construction cost of customers. In addition, We think that the distribution of car owners' charging on the expressway is normally distributed. Because many drivers will subconsciously recharge before entering or leaving the highway. So we built more charging stations in the middle of the highway.

Growth Model. Studies by Nathaniel et al. have shown that the average electric vehicle owner travels 44.7 miles per day [10], but can travel 220–310 miles after a slow charge. Therefore, when choosing the construction scheme of charging stations, we can consider the construction of more destination-charging stations. The data of electric vehicles from[1] show that the number of electric vehicles increased rapidly from 2012 to 2017. The results from [11] also showed that electric car ownership will increase rapidly in the first few years, But in the later stages of growth, the growth rate of electric vehicles will gradually slow down. This is consistent with the growth model of biological populations.

3 Quantity Prediction Model of Charging Station

According to our assumptions that total driving distance in one year keeps the same after cars are switched to all-electric vehicles, there must be some special mathematical connections between the number of gas stations and the charging stations. Considering the number of the total gas station, total sale of gas in one year, average number of fuel per car per day, average time of refueling fully at a time, average time of supercharging at a time, etc. And with the idea of **On Comparison**, we can get the following formulas:

$$C_{gas} = \alpha \times \frac{\frac{P_{tsg}}{P_{gpg}} \times \gamma}{365 \times T_{avg} \times N_{gas}} \tag{1}$$

$$D_{gas} = C_{gas} \times d_{gas} \tag{2}$$

$$k = \frac{\frac{D_{gas}}{t_{gas}}}{\frac{D_{sc}}{t_{sc}}} \tag{3}$$

$$N_{sc} = k \times N_{gas} \tag{4}$$

$$N_{ds} = 2 \times N_{sc} \tag{5}$$

$$N_c = N_{sc} + N_{dc} \tag{6}$$

Here we make α a coefficient referring to the ratio of energy provided by supercharging. According to the data we gathered laboriously from[2]. We approximately consider the number of destination-chargers is always twice more than superchargers. Thus, $\alpha = 0.33$, namely the energy provided by supercharging can enable a car to drive 33% distance of total in one year. P_{tsg} is total sale of gas in one year. P_{gpg} is gas price of per gallon. r is ratio of American gallon to liter, so, $r = 3.79$. T_{avg} is average number of refueling of per gas station at a time, and N_{gas} is total number of gas station, thus, C_{gas} means average number of fuel per car per day in unit of liter(L). d_{gas} is average allowed distance of per liter fuel. Thus, D_{gas} means average allowed distance of per time refueling. t_{gas}

---

[1] https://wattev2buy.com/global-ev-sales/south-korean-ev-market-ev-sales-south-korea/. Last accessed 4 July 2019.

[2] https://electrek.co/2017/04/15/tesla-destination-charging-network/.

is average time of refueling fully at a time, and $t_{gas} = 2$ min according to our assumption; t_{sc} is average time of supercharging at a time, and $t_{sc} = 30$ mins; D_{sc} is average allowed distance of supercharging per time, and $D_{sc} = 170$ miles; Thus, k is a ratio of the allowed distance by per unit time refueling to the allowed distance by per unit time supercharging. N_c is total number of charging stations. There are two types of stations, supercharging and destination-charging. N_{sc} is the number of the former, and N_{dc} is the number of the later. And we consider the ratio of gas efficiency to charging efficiency, namely k, as the proportion of supercharging stations. Besides, usually there are two chargers in a destination-charging station while eight in a supercharging station. What's more, the number of destination-chargers is approximately twice of superchargers. Therefore, the number of destination charging stations is eight times as many as supercharging stations, namely formula (1)–(6) And result is in Table 1.

4 Location Model for Charging Stations in Different Areas

Table 1. Result.

Variables	Value
C_{gas}	2.6
D_{gas}	15.6
k	1.377
N_{sc}	167158
N_{dc}	334316
N_c	501474

Function of Gradual Covering. Usually drivers prefer closer charging station considering of distance when they make choice. We define function of Gradual Covering as:

$$f(d_{ij}) = \begin{cases} 1 & d_{ij} \leq r \\ \frac{R-d_{ij}}{R-r} & r < d_{ij} < R \\ 0 & d_{ij} \geq R \end{cases} \quad (7)$$

where $i \in N$ (set of demand points, namely the driver's position), $j \in M$ (set of charging station construction spots), d_{ij} means the distance between demand point i and construction spot j, r means the shortest covering distance, R means the furthest covering distance. To simplify our model, we describe f by a linear ratio.

Covering Function. Covering function can help us define the coverage intensity for the current location.

$$g(X) = \sum_{i=0} f(d_{ij})x_j \tag{8}$$

where $X = x_1, ..., x_n, x_j \in 0, 1$, in detail

$$x_j = \begin{cases} 1 \; charging \; station \; in \; spot \; j \\ 0 \qquad\qquad\qquad\qquad else \end{cases} \tag{9}$$

Defining T as the threshold of covering. Therefore, our aim of Cooperative Covering model is to maximize the coverage weight of all demand points as far as possible. Namely the **objective function of Cooperative Covering model** is

$$z_1 = max\frac{\sum_i y_i}{|y|} \tag{10}$$

where $y_i \in \{0, 1\}$ and

$$y_j = \begin{cases} 1 \; when \; the \; weight \; of \; spot \; i \; is \; beyond \; T \\ 0 \qquad\qquad\qquad\qquad\qquad else \end{cases} \tag{11}$$

Minimum Construction Cost Model. We want to get a minimum construction cost under given constrains. So, the Objective Function is as follow:

$$z_2 = min \sum_{j=0} c_j x_j \tag{12}$$

and the constrains:

$$g(X) >= T$$

$$\sum_{j=0} c_i x_i <= C$$

where c_j is the cost of constructing in spot j, C is total construction budget, and T is the threshold of covering.

Model Solution & Results & Analyses. To solve a Bi-objective Programming Model, we need to turn double objectives into a single objective. We make w a coefficient to weigh z_1 and z_2. Thus, the solution is

$$min \, w \sum_{j} c_j x_j - (1 - w)\frac{\sum_i y_i}{|y|} \tag{13}$$

$$st. g(X) >= Ty_i \quad \forall i \in 1, .., n$$

$$\sum_{j=0} c_j x_j <= C$$

$$x_j \in \{0, 1\}$$
$$y_i \in \{0, 1\}$$

We select an area in Seoul for calculation to test the feasibility of our model. The results are showed in Fig. 1. The generation of demand points depends on the density of road network (where the density of road network is high, the demand points are correspondingly more). The building points are set as 8, and they are mainly located near the spots with high road network density. An orange point indicates not building at this point, and a blue one represents the establishment of a fast charging station at that point.

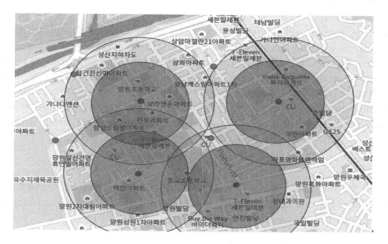

Fig. 1. Charging stations distribution of an area in Seoul. From the figure above, we can see that our model can achieve good results. This also reduces driver's queueing time.

5   Location Model of Supercharging Stations on Expressway Based on Queue Theory

Usually the driving distance is long on highway, and people are in a hurry. Thus, the measure of building supercharging stations on highway is especially important. Here, we just consider one direction only. The result of the other direction can be obtained in the same way. Analogous to the service area on expressway, we find that the setting of the service area generally conforms to the principle of continuous driving. Considering the total distance that the vehicle can travel before an intersection is the limit distance between the service areas. However, generally, the distance between the service areas will be less than this limit distance. From the existing setting of freeway rest station in Korea, the distance between rest stations is set at 30 km [6]. Besides, the expressway is not as complex as the urban network, so the distribution of supercharging stations can be established through equidistant partition. Thus, we adopt following model when setting the distance between charging stations:

$$d_e = \min\{\frac{L}{\frac{L}{0.25d_{EL}}}, 30\} \tag{14}$$

where d_e is the distance between stations, L is total length of expressway, d_{EL} is the distance EV can drive after once supercharging. Here

$$d_{EL} = 170 \, \text{miles} = 272 \, \text{km}$$

Clearly, $d_e = 30$ km. Considering the specialty of expressway, so we think supercharging stations should be set inside the rest area. We suppose a rest station can allow the construction of several fast charging stations. By setting a reasonable distance, we can allow drivers on highway to achieve charging. And what matters more is waiting time. Too few supercharging stations on expressway will make drivers to wait for a long time and lead to irritable psychology, which will make people lose confidence in electric vehicles. On contrary, too many stations maybe bring waste of resource. Therefore, to balance these two conditions, we consider modeling based on Queuing Theory. We assume Q_t as vehicle flow rate in sometime. The possibility of demander's choice satisfies normal distribution

$$f(x) = \frac{1}{\sqrt{2\pi}\sigma} exp(-\frac{(x - \mu_0)^2}{2\sigma^2}) \tag{15}$$

where $\mu_0 = \frac{L}{2}$, and L is the total length of highway. Because of Pauta Criterion, the possibility of x out of $(\mu_0 - 3\sigma, \mu_0 + 3\sigma)$ is smaller than 0.3%. Thus, setting $\sigma = \frac{L}{6}$ can reflect the demand. And the model changes to

$$f(x) = \frac{6}{\sqrt{2\pi}L} exp(-\frac{18(x - \frac{L}{2})^2}{L^2}) \tag{16}$$

The probability of building charging station in x_{j+1} is

$$P_{j+1} = \frac{\int_0^{x_{j+1}} f(x)dx - \int_0^{x_j} f(x)dx}{\int_0^L f(x)dx} \tag{17}$$

The number of drivers in x_{j+1} is num_{j+1}, and $num_{j+1} = Q_t \times P_{j+1}$. We adopt $M/M/n/m/m$ model(Multi-Service window closed queuing model) [8], and we assume the service intensity $\mu = 30$ min per car, arrival strength $\lambda = 40$ mins per car, capacity of charging station j as m_j, the number of cars in need as num_j. To simplify the calculation, considering there are 8 chargers in a charging station, we make

$$m_j = \lceil \frac{num_j}{8} \rceil \tag{18}$$

According to regularity condition, we have

$$p_{o_j} = \left(\sum_{l=0}^{n_j-1} C_{m_j}^l \rho_1^l + \sum_{l=n_j}^{m_j} \frac{c_{m_j}^l l!}{(n_j)! n_j (l - n_j)} p_1^l \right)^{-1} \tag{19}$$

where $\rho_1 = \frac{\lambda}{\mu} = \frac{2}{3}$, $C_m^l = \frac{m!}{l!(m-l)!}$, n_j is the number of supercharging stations in j_{th} rest area, $p_{0_j} j$ is the probability of no any car in need in j_{th} supercharging station. The average queue length of j_{th} station L_{q_j} meets

$$L_{q_j} = \sum_{l=n_j+1}^{m_j} \frac{(l-n_j)c_{m_j}^l l! \rho_1^l}{(n_j)! n_j^{l-n_j}} p_{0_j} \tag{20}$$

Under the condition of statistical balance, we have $\lambda_e = \bar{\mu}$, for simplification, we could make $\mu = 30$ mins per car, then we can calculate the average waiting time W_{q_j} as

$$W_{q_j} = \frac{L_{q_j}}{\lambda_e} = \frac{L_{q_j}}{30} \tag{21}$$

Therefore, we propose a bi-objective programming of minimizing average total waiting time and total building cost. To make it easier to solve this bi-objective programming, we define a coefficient of weight to skillfully change it into a single objective programming. Finally, the objective is

$$\min \omega \sum_{j=0} W_{q_j} - (1-\omega) \sum_{j=0} cn_j \tag{22}$$

$$0 <= W_{q_j} <= t$$

$$\sum_{j=0} cn_j <= C$$

$$n_j >= 1$$

where ω is a coefficient of weight, W_{q_j} is the average waiting time of j_{th} station, c is building cost (here we assume the cost of each charger is the same), n_j is the number of supercharging stations built in j_{th} rest station. $j \in M$(set of charging station construction spots), C is the building budget.

We take Yeongdong Expressway to analyze. We find that there should be two supercharging station in first rest station, and three supercharging stations in second rest station from origin. The result is the same on the other side. We can see clearly in Fig. 2.

6 Growth Plan on Charging Station Construction and Development of Electric Vehicles

Electric vehicles emerge in these years, and South Korean government announced its EV incentive program in 2011. There is promising market for EV in South Korea. The EV sales from 2012 to 2017[16] are in Fig. 3. According to Fig. 4, from the proportion of EV sales to total new car sales in each region, we can see that all the countries as a whole will vigorously develop electric vehicles to replace fuel vehicles in 25 years from 2015 to 2040. The increase of EV sales express particularly obvious over the 15 years from 2025 to 2040, which is slowing

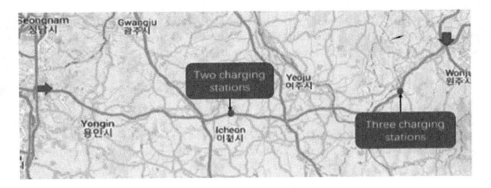

Fig. 2. The supercharging stations planning of Yeongdong Expressway

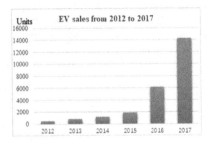

Fig. 3. EV sales from 2012 to 2017 From the figure above, we can see that in the past six years, the sales of South Korean electric vehicles have rapidly grown from 455 to 14,234.

Fig. 4. Annual predicted sale percentage of electric vehicles in various countries from [11]

down after 2040. This is similar to a biological growth pattern in which species migrate to a new ecosystem (non-ideal environment). Therefore, to predict the future purchases of electric vehicles in the next 20 years by 2040 we establish the following model:

$$s(x) = \frac{a}{1 + b^{-x+c}} + d \tag{23}$$

where a, b, c, d are constants, and x is a variable related to time. Because our data starts from 2012, we make $x = t - 2011$, where t refers to year. Differentiating formula (22), we get

$$s'(x) = \frac{a\log(b)b^{c-x}}{(b^{-x+c} + 1)^2} \tag{24}$$

$s'(x)$ reaches maximum when $x = c$. Around 2025, the sale proportion of EV starts to grow rapidly, and the growth rate reaches maximum in about 2032. Thus, we can set $c = 20$. When it's up to 2040 or so, the sale proportion of EV generally achieve 50% as a whole. We find the specific sale of cars in South Korea

Table 2. Sale in 2040 under different values of b.

b	EV sales($\times 10^4$)
1.25	42
1.275	53
1.3	69
1.325	89
1.35	110

is 1,750,000[3]. Adjusting the value of b, we acquire corresponding sale in 2040. The results are displayed in Table 2. Meanwhile, considering the popularity of EV in the future, the manufacture of fuel vehicles must decrease. To meet 50% of the new vehicle sale, compared with 1,750,000, we select $b = 1.325$. Ultimately, we obtain the final model by fitting as

$$s(x) = \frac{9.375 \times 10^5}{1 + 1.325^{20-x}} - 5828 \tag{25}$$

7 Classification Model Based on K-means

Our plan of evolving charging network is applicable for Australia, China, Indonesia, Saudi Arabia, and Singapore before achieving 50% electric vehicles on road. We can obtain a good development plan by combining the number of cars in various countries, the trend of electric vehicles in recent years, the specific situation of urban and rural structure, the scale and distribution of existing charging stations, and adjusting the existing model structure appropriately. If the development of EV continues, we need to analyze with the specific development environment of electric vehicles in various countries. We consider following indexes.

Expenditures on R&D (Research and Development). The scale and intensity of R&D activities are generally used to reflect a country's scientific and technological strength and core competitiveness. However, for the wider popularization of electric vehicles, battery technology innovation and other science and technology are essential to reduce user's daily expenses, so as to facilitate the travel of users, finally to enhance the market competitiveness.

GDP(Gross Domestic Product). GDP is often regarded as a measure of national (or regional) economic condition. The increase of GDP will inevitably lead to the growth of consumption. For countries with high GDP, the development of electric vehicles will be smoother.

---

[3] https://www.motorgraph.com/news/articleView.html?idxno=11376. Last accessed 4 July 2019.

GINI. GINI is usually used to measure the gap between the rich and the poor in a country, but the price of electric vehicles is generally higher than that of fuel cars. So countries with smaller gap between the rich and the poor is easier to popularize electric vehicles.

Gas and Electricity Price. When the cost of charging is lower than that of a refueling for the same driving distance, it can also contribute to the popularity of electric vehicles.

Energy Consumption. For countries with high energy costs, environmental issue is likely to be more pronounced. Introducing cleaner energy to replace the old becomes even more necessary. Thus, this index also has the effect on promoting the popularity of electric vehicles. Therefore, we select R&D, GDP, Gini, Electricity and Gas Price, and Energy Consumption as our criteria for choosing different growth networks. Here we can think that these indicators can promote the development of charging stations to some extent. But the number and distribution of chargers in the future are difficult to predict accurately, so we do not include the scale distribution of charging stations in the analysis parameters. The compassion among countries is in Fig. 5. It is not reliable to distinguish different types of countries subjectively. Data processing is in need. Therefore, we normalize the data first

$$x = \frac{x - x_{min}}{x_{max} - x_{min}} \qquad (26)$$

After normalization, the common attributes of each column are mapped to [0–1], which can be converted into dimensionless values and improve the accuracy of K-means model. We classify the countries into three categories by K-means, and the result is in Table 3. We can find the development environment of Australia, Singapore, and Korea is close. They are generally ahead of other countries in GDP per capita, expenditures on R&D per capita, and energy consumption, while their GINI is relevantly lower. Compared to other types of countries, the development environment of these three countries is very likely to realize all-electric vehicles. For China, GDP, expenditures on R&D, and the relative proportion between gas price and electricity price are far ahead of the other countries. But Chinese GDP per capita is not high enough, meanwhile GINI is large. Although it is difficult to be fully popularized, China is a development environment in which widespread popularization could be achieved. Besides, Indonesian GINI is small but GDP per capita there is the lowest. At the same time, China and Indonesia also has the least R&D investment, so countries of class 2 and 3 can only achieve 50% of the market coverage of electric vehicles.

Proportions of each index in different countries

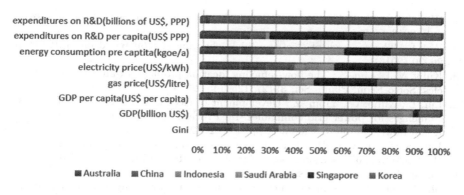

Fig. 5. Proportion of corresponding index of each country. We can see the difference between countries is great.

Table 3. Category of countries.

Country	Class
Australia	1
Singapore	1
South Korea	1
China	2
Indonesia	2
Saudi Arabic	3

8   Conclusion

We adopt the idea of on Comparison based on the similarity between gas stations and the supercharging stations, to calculate the number of fully electrified charging stations through the number of gas stations and the distance the fuel vehicles travel in one year. That avoids overfitting for regression prediction when using existing data only. Due to the differences in geography, we analyze urban and suburban areas (represented by expressway) separately, which makes the model more accurate. We do prediction based on existing researches. Combining practical rules, we adopt Logistic Growth model, which is more in line with the laws of electric vehicle development.

Acknowledgements. This work is supported by Major Scientific and Technological Special Project of Guizhou Province(20183002), and I have learned a lot from the writing of this paper. I would like to thank professor Qiu and Song for their tireless teaching and correcting my mistakes.

References

1. Wikipedia. https://en.wikipedia.org/wiki/Tesla_Supercharger. Last accessed 4 July 2019
2. Wu, L.: The research of electric vehicle charging station based on GMCLP, pp. 26–30 (2016)
3. Kuby, M.J., Lim, S.: The flow-refueling location problem for alternative-fuel vehicles. Socio-Econ. Plann. Sci. **39**(2), 125–145 (2015)
4. Lili, L., Xubo, G., Yibin, Z.: Development of electric vehicles: opportunities and challenges for power grid companies. In: Proceedings of the Fifth China International Power Supply Conference, pp. 1–7 (2012)
5. Lim, S., Kuby, M.J.: Heuristic algorithmsfor siting alternative fuel stations using the flow-refueling location model. Eur. J. Oper. Res. **204**(1), 51–61 (2010)
6. Zhang, Y.: Chinese Expressway (2015)
7. Shi, D., Zhou, J.: Comparison of service areas on expressway at home and abroad (2016)
8. Chuanji, L.: Queuing Theory, 2nd edn. Beijing Youdian University, Beijing (2009)
9. South Korea Gasoline Prices. https://tradingeconomics.com/south-korea/gasoline-prices. Last accessed 4 July 2019
10. Pearre, N.S., Kempton, W., Guensler, R.L., Elango, V.V.: Electric vehicles: how much range is required for a day's driving? Transp. Res. Part C: Emerg. Technol. **19**(6), 1171–1184 (2011)
11. Figure source. https://about.bnef.com/. Last accessed 2 Feb 2018
12. Icct. https://www.theicct.org/blogs/staff/promoting-electric-vehicles-in-korea. Last accessed 4 July 2019
13. Aju Business Daily. http://www.ajudaily.com/. Last accessed 4 July 2019
14. Xinhua. http://inf.315che.com/n/2007_01/29650/. Last accessed 4 July 2019
15. South Korea's ministry of land and oceans. http://www.mofcom.gov.cn/aarticle/i/dxfw/cj/201104/20110407486496.html. Last accessed 4 July 2019
16. Nie, L.: Multi-objective progressive coverage model and solution for the temporary medical waste storage site selection. China Population Res. Environ. **2015**(S1), 110–112 (2018)
17. Zhou, Y.: Journal **2**(5), 99–110 (2016)
18. Li, Z.: Research on urban EV charging network planning and operation based on traffic behavior, Shandong University (2014)

Boundary Detector Encoder and Decoder with Soft Attention for Video Captioning

Tangming Chen[1,2]([✉]), Qike Zhao[1,2], and Jingkuan Song[1,2]

[1] Guizhou Provincial Key Laboratory of Public Big Data,
GuiZhou University, Guiyang 550025, Guizhou, China
tangmingchen8@gmail.com
[2] University of Electronic Science and Technology of China, Chengdu, China

Abstract. The use of Recurrent Neural Networks and Convolutional Neural Networks for video captioning has received widespread attention, since the deep learning has developed rapidly. Based on classical encoder-decoder approach, we modify the encoding networks and decoding networks to improve the performance of the entire networks. In this paper, we introduce an encoding scheme that can detect the hierarchical structure of the input video. What's more, we use soft attention mechanism which can learn to automatically select the relevant input frames from the input video to generate the description of the input video. Extensive experiments are conducted on two datasets: the Microsoft Video Description Corpus and the MSR-Video To Text. Three metrics, BLEU@4, METEOR and CIDEr are used to evaluate our approach. Experimental results demonstrate the effectiveness of our approach.

Keywords: LSTM · Boundary detector · Soft attention

1 Introduction

As we enter the information age, video devices such as cameras are constantly updated. Videos become a major way for people to communicate daily and massive video information is constantly transmitted. However, complex information in the videos makes them hard to be fully used.

Video captioning, the machine automatically generates natural language to describe the video, brings a keen interest to researchers dedicated to video research. The development of deep learning promotes the progress of video captioning, which is of great significance to society. Indeed, video captioning has many applications in human-robot interaction, automatic video and surveillance. It can be leveraged to help visually impaired people to get the content of a video and to generate automatic subtitles.

Video captioning research started with the classical template [11] which detects separately Subject, Verb and Object, then captions were generated through a sentence template. However, the approach can produce a rigid captioning and cannot satisfy the richness of natural language. At the same time,

J. Song and X. Zhu (Eds.): APWeb-WAIM 2019 Workshops, LNCS 11809, pp. 105–115, 2019.
https://doi.org/10.1007/978-3-030-33982-1_9

the advent of deep learning has greatly promoted the advancements in CV and NLP. Hence, latest approaches almost use encoder-decoder scheme [16,21] that encodes the visual features with 2D/3D-CNN and use LSTM/GRU to temporally generate sentences.

Early research on video captioning mostly focused on domain specific short video clips with limited vocabularies of objects and activities [3,13]. The main differences of the approaches that use encoder-decoder framework are the different types of CNNs in encoding scheme and the different language models in decoding networks. Later methods were progressed by adding some modules on the standard encoder-decoder framework. [21] proposed a neural structure used in both the video encoding stage and sentence decoding stage. They used a stacked LSTM to encode the input video. Interestingly, they used the same stacked LSTM to generate sentence. The advantages of the approach are that they can keep the sequential nature of input video and the network can use same parameters in the two stages. The framework has been widely followed by other works and already applied to machine translation [19].

Recently, researchers improved the encoder-decoder framework by significantly modifying their components. [2] paid attention to the encoder scheme and proposed a hierarchical boundary-aware neural encoder which could identify discontinuity points between video frames. [25] proposed a temporal attention mechanism that learned to select the relevant frames to the decoder by focusing on the sentence decoder. Many methods based on various attention mechanisms [7,8,18,25] have been successfully used in video captioning. Encouraged by [2,25], we use a boundary detector [2] to improve the encoding scheme and employ a temporal attention mechanism [25] in decoder stage to generate sentences.

2   Method

2.1   Boundary Detector

In this paper, we use a new video encoding scheme which can detect temporal discontinuities, such as action or appearance changes, to generate description. Figure 1 shows the structure: the features extracted from the input frames by ResNet152 are fed into the boundary detector module. When the action or appearance of the input video changes, the boundary detector scheme will automatically modify the connectivity of the LSTM layer. Another LSTM layer is adopted to get the features of video clip whose last frame is regarded as a boundary, then we can get the features of the whole video at the end of the video by LSTM layer.

Given an input video, the boundary detector will take a sequence of features $(x_1, x_2, ..., x_n)$ as input and output a sequence of vectors $(s_1, s_2, ..., s_n)$. In the encoder, the connectivity state of the LSTM layer will change when the input and the hidden state of the layer change. Therefore, the boundary detector is regarded as an activation rather than a non learnable hyperparameter.

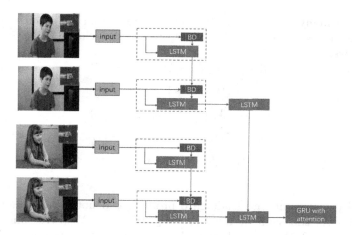

Fig. 1. Illustration of our framework. We use a boundary detector (BD) to detect the temporal discontinuities of the input video. When the detector detects the time boundary, the hidden state will be passed to the next LSTM layer rather than the next time step. At last, we use a GRU layer with soft attention to generate the description of the input video.

At each time step, the choice of the encoder is to transfer the memory cell content and hidden state to next time step or reinitialize them, thus interrupting the seamless update and the processing of input sequence. What decides the result is boundary detector cell which allows the encoder independently to handle video blocks of different lengths. The boundaries of each chunk are determined by a learnable function which depends on the input and not a determined formula. Formally, the boundary detector S_t is calculated as a linear combination of the current input and hidden state. The function τ, which is a combination of a sigmoid function and a step function, can be represented by the following expression:

$$S_t = \tau(V^T \cdot (W_{si}X_t + W_{sh}h_{t-1} + b_s)) \tag{1}$$

where X_t is the input frame, W_{si}, W_{sh} are learned weights, b_s is learned bias, V^T is a learned vector and h_{t-1} is the hidden state of last time step.

Given the current result of boundary detector, we can use the following substitutions to update the network hidden state and memory cell which are transferred to the next time step.

$$h_{t-1} = h_{t-1} \cdot (1 - S_t) \tag{2}$$

$$c_{t-1} = c_{t-1} \cdot (1 - S_t) \tag{3}$$

If the boundary detector S_t is 1, the hidden state will be passed to the next layer which used to get the feature of the video clip rather than the next time step.

There are many proposed LSTM architecture [9, 10, 12, 17] which are sightly different in their structure. In this paper, we use the scheme [10]. Its equations are as follows.

$$i_t = \sigma(W_{ix}X_t + W_{ih}h_{t-1} + b_i) \tag{4}$$

$$f_t = \sigma(W_{fx}X_t + W_{fh}h_{t-1} + b_f) \tag{5}$$

$$g_t = \phi(W_{gx}X_t + W_{gh}h_{t-1} + b_g) \tag{6}$$

$$o_t = \phi(W_{fx}X_t + W_{fh}h_{t-1} + b_f) \tag{7}$$

$$c_t = f_t \odot c_{t-1} + i_t \odot g_t \tag{8}$$

$$h_t = o_t \odot \phi(c_t) \tag{9}$$

where $\odot$ is the element-wise Hadamard product, ϕ denotes the hyperbolic tangent tanh, σ is the sigmoid function, $W_{ix}, W_{fx}, W_{gx}, W_{ih}, W_{fh}$ and W_{gh} are learned matrices, b_i, b_f, b_g are learned biases vectors, X_t is the input data. The hidden state h_t and memory cell c_t are initialized to zero. The input gate i_t controls how the current input should be passed to current memory cell c_t. f_t is the forget gate which is applied to control what the cell forget from the last memory cell c_{t-1}. The output gate o_t decides whether the current memory cell is output. Figure 2 shows a schema of the boundary detector.

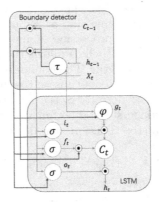

Fig. 2. The scheme of the boundary detector

According to the above equations, the boundary detector will get a different length series of outputs$(s_1, s_2, ..., s_m)$, where m is the number of video boundary. Each of the outputs represents the content of a video segment. The outputs are passed to another LSTM layer to build a hierarchical representation of the input video. At last, the last hidden state of the additional LSTM layer can be used as the feature vector of the whole video.

2.2   Attention

In this paper, we adopt the soft attention mechanism that is proposed in [25]. The soft attention mechanism allows the decoder to weight the feature vector $V = (v_1, v_2, ..., v_n)$ of each video frame so that the decoder can pay more attention to the input frames related to input of decoder. The decoder can get more precise input data than the decoder without attention mechanism, so we can produce more natural captioning.

We get the feature vector of each input frames by the encoder and the weight distribution e_t of the input video frames can be obtained by the following equation:

$$e_t = W^T \phi(W_a h_{t-1} + U_a V_i + b_a) \tag{10}$$

where W^T, W_a and U_a are learned weight matrix, b_a denotes a learned bias vector, h_{t-1} is the hidden state at last time step, V_i represents the feature of the entire input video which is got by concatenating the feature of each video frames and ϕ is the tanh function.

Through the above formula, we can obtain the correlation score e_t of all input frames, then we normalize e_t to get the probability distributions p_t of the input video frames by a softmax function. Finally, we multiply the obtained probability distributions p_t and the features of the whole video V_i to get the final input of decoder F. The equation is as follows:

$$F = V_i \odot \theta(e_t) \tag{11}$$

2.3   Training

The function τ is a combination of a sigmoid function and a step function so that we need a special training method to train the encoder. First, the boundary detector S_t is regard as a stochastic neuron [15]. In particular, we use a stochastic version of function τ. Formally, τ can be computed as follows during the forward propagation of training stage.

$$\tau(x) = \begin{cases} 0, & \sigma(x) < Z, Z \sim U[0,1] \\ 1, & otherwise \end{cases} \tag{12}$$

where $U[0, 1]$ is uniform distribution on [0,1]. This ensures that the boundary detector S_t is stochastic and its probability of 0 or 1 is proportional to the value of the input $\sigma(x)$.

During the backward pass, since the derivative of the step function is zero, we cannot use the standard back propagation. To solve the problem, we apply the approach suggested by Bengio et al. [5]. The method is based on the idea that if the network uses a differentiable approximation in backward propagation, the network can apply discrete operations in forward propagation. In our work, the derivative of τ used in backward pass is simply the derivative of the sigmoid function.

$$\frac{\partial \tau}{\partial x}(x) = \sigma(x)(1 - \sigma(x)) \tag{13}$$

At test phase, we employ the deterministic version of step function (Eq. 14). Therefore, the number of video segments detected by the boundary detector encoder is random during training and is deterministic during the test.

$$\tau(x) = \begin{cases} 0, \ \sigma(x) < 0.5 \\ 1, \ otherwise \end{cases} \qquad (14)$$

2.4   Sentence Generation

As for the decoder, we use GRU which is a variant of LSTM. According to the boundary detector encoder and the attention mechanism, the feature vector F of input video frame at current time step can be obtained. What's more, the video captioning $(y_1, y_2, ..., y_t)$ corresponding to the video is encoded with one-hot vectors. In order to get natural captioning, we use scheduled sampling [4] in decoding. The technique is applied to choose whether the input word is the ground-truth word or a word predicted in the previous time step, which is considered as a comprehensive consideration of the training process and testing phase. In particular, if the random number is greater than the threshold T (Eq. 15), we will use ground-truth word rather than predicted word at current time step. The hidden state and general feature that contains feature vector F and input word vector are entered into GRU to predict the word.

$$T = max(0.6, (K/(K + exp(epoch/K)))) \qquad (15)$$

where epoch is the number of network iterations, K is set to 24.

Our decoder gradually adjusts the first t words of the caption and is trained to produce the next word of the captioning until it predicts $< END >$ or the length of predicted words is greater 30. The loss function which we optimize is as follows:

$$Loss = -\sum_{k=1}^{N} \log q_k \qquad (16)$$

where N is the dimension of output and q_k represents the predicted probability of the k-th neuron.

3   Experimental Setup

3.1   Datasets

Microsoft Video Description Corpus (MSVD). The Microsoft Video Description Corpus [6] contains 1970 YouTube video clips that are 10 to 25 seconds long and each video is labeled with about 40 English sentences. As the previous works [11,22] did, we divide the dataset into consecutive video groups by index number:1200 for training, 100 for validation and 670 for testing.

Microsoft Research - Video to Text (MSR-VTT) the Microsoft Research - Video to Text is achieved by collecting 257 popular queries. It offers 10K video clips for a total of 41.2 h and 200K clip sentences covering the most comprehensive categories. As done in previous work [24], we split the dataset in contiguous groups of videos by index number: 6513 for training, 497 for validation and 2990 for test.

3.2 Metrics

We use three popular evaluation metrics:BLEU [14], METEOR [1] and CIDEr [20]. BLEU uses n-gram to calculate the co-occurrence frequency of ground-true sentence and predicted sentence. Like most of previous work, we use 4-gram to evaluate the sentence produced by our network. METEOR is based on BLEU with some improvements, adding the relationship between the generated sentence and the ground-true sentence. CIDEr, finally, treats each sentence as a document and calculates the cosine angle of the TF-IDF vector, which gives the similarity between the predicted sentence and the reference sentence.

4 Experimental Results

4.1 Ablation Study

In order to clearly understand the roles of the boundary detector and attention mechanism, we have done three sets of experiments on both MSVD and MSR-VTT: an experiment with a boundary detector and attention mechanism (BD_attention), an experiment with a boundary detector but no attention mechanism (BD), an experiment without a boundary detector and attention mechanism (BD_NO).

Table 1. Results on MSVD

	BLEU@4	METEOR	CIDEr
BD_NO	39.1	30.0	61.7
BD	41.4	30.9	65.8
BD_attention	44.1	32.12	70.1

Table 1 shows the results on MSVD. First of all, to understand the role of the boundary detector, we compare BD and BD_NO. The result of BD outperforms the result of BD_NO on the three metrics. Specifically, BD is 5.9%, 3.0%, 6.6% higher than BD_NO on BLEU@4, METEOR and CIDEr. Secondly, comparing BD_attention and BD, we can clearly realize that the attention mechanism can make the sentences generated by our network closer to the ground-true sentences. For reference, BD_attention achieves a 6.5% BLEU@4, 3.9% METEOR, 6.5% CIDEr.

The performance on MSR-VTT is reported in Table 2. The role of boundary detector can be obtained by comparing BD and BD_NO. For reference, BD reports a 0.5% BLEU@4, 0.7% METEOR, 2.9% CIDEr. According to BD and BD_attention, we observe that the attention mechanism plays an import role in our framework. In particular, the improvement of the attention mechanism is 4.3% BLEU@4, 0.4% METEOR, 3.5% CIDEr.

Table 2. Results on MSR-VTT

	BLEU@4	METEOR	CIDEr
BD_NO	36.9	26.4	38.5
BD	37.1	26.6	39.6
BD_attention	38.7	26.7	41.0

4.2 Compared Approaches

On the dataset MSVD, we have chosen three advanced methods in recent years to compare with our method. Temporal attention (SA) [25] uses a decoder with an attention mechanism and extracts feature from GoogleNet and a 3D CNN. S2VT [21] employs a stacked LSTMs for decoder and encoder. LSTM-YT [21] applies a CNN encoder which uses mean pooling for downsamping to extract the feature of the input video.

Table 3. Comparison with others on MSVD

	BLEU@4	METEOR	CIDEr
SA	41.9	26.6	51.67
S2VT	–	29.8	–
LSTM-YT	33.3	29.1	–
BD_attention (ours)	44.1	32.1	70.1

The results on this dataset are shown in Table 3. It is obvious that our method has better performance than others. We especially focus on the approach SA which also uses an attention mechanism. The BLEU@4, METEOR and CIDEr for BD_attention(ours) can reach 44.1, 32.1, 70.1, making the relative improvement over SA by 5.3%, 8.4%, 35.7%, respectively. The results imply the advantage of our boundary detector.

On the MSR-VTT dataset, we again consider SA and LSTM-YT which are both used in [18]. We also choose two other approaches: M3 [23] which builds a textual and visual shared memory to model the long-term visual-textual dependency, hLSTMat [18] that uses the temporal attention to select specific frames

Table 4. Comparison with others on MSR-VTT

	BLEU@4	METEOR	CIDEr
SA	36.6	26.1	–
M3	38.1	26.6	–
LSTM-YT	35.8	25.3	–
hLSTMat	38.3	26.3	–
BD_attention (ours)	38.7	26.7	41.0

to generate the words, while the adjusted temporal attention is for deciding whether to depend on the visual information or the language context information. As it can be noticed in Table 4, the results across BELU@4 and METEOR point that our BD_attention shows better performance than other runs.

Figures 3 and 4 present a few examples on MSVD, MSR-VTT respectively. It is obvious that the sentences generated by BD_attention can describe the video well.

BD_attention: a person is spreading butter on a piece of bread
GT: a guy is spreading butter on bread

BD_atention: a man is talking on a phone
GT: a man is speaking on a phone

Fig. 3. Sampling on MSVD

BD_attention: a man is showing how to fold a piece of paper
GT: a man is folding pieces of paper

BD_attention: a person is skiing down a snowy mountain
GT: person is skiing on the mountain filled with snow

Fig. 4. Sampling on MSR-VTT

5   Conclusion

In this paper, we use a boundary detector encoder which can discover the hierarchical structure of the video and employ a decoder with attention mechanism. Experiments on MSVD and MSR-VTT show that our method is comparable to the state-of-the-art models. In the future, we will further improve the boundary detector.

Acknowledgments. This work is supported by Major Scientific and Technological Special Project of Guizhou Province (20183002).

References

1. Banerjee, S., Lavie, A.: METEOR: an automatic metric for MT evaluation with improved correlation with human judgments. In: Proceedings of the ACL Workshop on Intrinsic and Extrinsic Evaluation Measures for Machine Translation and/or Summarization, pp. 65–72 (2005)
2. Baraldi, L., Grana, C., Cucchiara, R.: Hierarchical boundary-aware neural encoder for video captioning. In: Proceedings of the IEEE Conference on Computer Vision and Pattern Recognition, pp. 1657–1666 (2017)
3. Barbu, A., et al.: Video in sentences out. arXiv preprint arXiv:1204.2742 (2012)
4. Bengio, S., Vinyals, O., Jaitly, N., Shazeer, N.: Scheduled sampling for sequence prediction with recurrent neural networks. In: Advances in Neural Information Processing Systems, pp. 1171–1179 (2015)
5. Bengio, Y., Léonard, N., Courville, A.: Estimating or propagating gradients through stochastic neurons for conditional computation. arXiv preprint arXiv:1308.3432 (2013)
6. Chen, D.L., Dolan, W.B.: Collecting highly parallel data for paraphrase evaluation. In: Proceedings of the 49th Annual Meeting of the Association for Computational Linguistics: Human Language Technologies, vol. 1, pp. 190–200 (2011)
7. Fang, H., et al.: From captions to visual concepts and back. In: Proceedings of the IEEE Conference on Computer Vision and Pattern Recognition, pp. 1473–1482 (2015)
8. Gao, L., Guo, Z., Zhang, H., Xu, X., Shen, H.T.: Video captioning with attention-based LSTM and semantic consistency. IEEE Trans. Multimed. **19**(9), 2045–2055 (2017)
9. Gers, F.A., Schmidhuber, J., Cummins, F.: Learning to forget: continual prediction with LSTM (1999)
10. Graves, A., Mohamed, A., Hinton, G.: Speech recognition with deep recurrent neural networks. In: 2013 IEEE International Conference on Acoustics, Speech and Signal Processing, pp. 6645–6649 (2013)
11. Guadarrama, S., et al.: Youtube2text: recognizing and describing arbitrary activities using semantic hierarchies and zero-shot recognition. In: Proceedings of the IEEE International Conference on Computer Vision, pp. 2712–2719 (2013)
12. Hochreiter, S., Schmidhuber, J.: Long short-term memory. Neural Comput. **9**(8), 1735–1780 (1997)
13. Khan, M.U.G., Gotoh, Y.: Describing video contents in natural language. In: Proceedings of the Workshop on Innovative Hybrid Approaches to the Processing of Textual Data, pp. 27–35 (2012)
14. Papineni, K., Roukos, S., Ward, T., Zhu, W.-J.: BLEU: a method for automatic evaluation of machine translation. In: Proceedings of the 40th Annual Meeting on Association for Computational Linguistics, pp. 311–318 (2002)
15. Raiko, T., Berglund, M., Alain, G., Dinh, L.: Techniques for learning binary stochastic feedforward neural networks. arXiv preprint arXiv:1406.2989 (2014)
16. Rohrbach, A., et al.: Movie description. Int. J. Comput. Vis. **123**(1), 94–120 (2017)
17. Schmidhuber, J., Wierstra, D., Gagliolo, M., Gomez, F.: Training recurrent networks by evolino. Neural Comput. **19**(3), 757–779 (2007)
18. Song, J., Guo, Z., Gao, L., Liu, W., Zhang, D., Shen, H.T.: Hierarchical LSTM with adjusted temporal attention for video captioning. arXiv preprint arXiv:1706.01231 (2017)

19. Sutskever, I., Vinyals, O., Le, Q.V.: Sequence to sequence learning with neural networks. In: Advances in Neural Information Processing Systems, pp. 3104–3112 (2014)
20. Vedantam, R., Lawrence Zitnick, C., Parikh, D.: CIDEr: consensus-based image description evaluation. In: Proceedings of the IEEE Conference on Computer Vision and Pattern Recognition, pp. 4566–4575 (2015)
21. Venugopalan, S., Rohrbach, M., Donahue, J., Mooney, R., Darrell, T., Saenko, K.: Sequence to sequence-video to text. In: Proceedings of the IEEE International Conference on Computer Vision, pp. 4534–4542 (2015)
22. Venugopalan, S., Xu, H., Donahue, J., Rohrbach, M., Mooney, R., Saenko, K.: Translating videos to natural language using deep recurrent neural networks. arXiv preprint arXiv:1412.4729 (2014)
23. Wang, J., Wang, W., Huang, Y., Wang, L., Tan, T.: M3: multimodal memory modelling for video captioning. In: Proceedings of the IEEE Conference on Computer Vision and Pattern Recognition, pp. 7512–7520 (2018)
24. Xu, J., Mei, T., Yao, T., Rui, Y.: MSR-VTT: a large video description dataset for bridging video and language. In: Proceedings of the IEEE Conference on Computer Vision and Pattern Recognition, pp. 5288–5296 (2016)
25. Yao, L., et al.: Describing videos by exploiting temporal structure. In: Proceedings of the IEEE International Conference on Computer Vision, pp. 4507–4515 (2015)

Author Index

Printed in the United States
By Bookmasters